Beyond Vinyl:

The Rock & Roll Saga Continues

By

Donald Riggio

Nancy,
Once again my thanks for your loyalty to my work.

Much love,
Donald Riggio
4/15

This book is a work of fiction. Though some characters described herein interact with real persons there was no intention on the part of the author to portray these interactions as factual. However with respect to historic events every effort was made to be as accurate as possible. The opinions expressed in this manuscript are solely the opinions of the author and do not represent the opinions or thoughts of the publisher. The author has represented and warranted full ownership and/or legal right to publish all the materials in this book.

Beyond Vinyl
The Rock and Roll Saga Continues
All Rights Reserved.
Copyright © 2012 Donald Riggio

This book may not be reproduced, transmitted, or stored in whole or in part by any means, including graphic, electronic, or mechanical without the express written consent of the publisher except in the case of brief quotations embodied in critical articles and reviews.

PRINTED IN THE UNITED STATES OF AMERICA

What People Are Saying About Beyond Vinyl:

"In my twenty-seven years as the host of the *DooWop Shop* on WCBS-FM radio in New York City, and my appearances as Master of Ceremonies at countless oldies shows, I've worked with some of the greatest artists performing the music of the 50s and 60s. It is fitting that someone would come along and capture the same sense of excitement with the written word. With his novels, *Seven-Inch Vinyl* and now the sequel *Beyond Vinyl*, Donald Riggio has done just that."

Don K. Reed

"A seamless sequel. Like a good ballad from the 60s, *Beyond Vinyl* continues to keep the music alive and well. Donald has done it again."

Kenny Vance

"With his sequel, *Beyond Vinyl*, Donald Riggio once again transports us to the golden days of rock and roll and *beyond*. An array of familiar, new and sometimes surprising characters take us on a journey the reader will never forget. I predict back to back #1 hits for this author."

Jon "Bowzer" Bauman

"The adventure continues. Just as he did in *Seven-Inch Vinyl*, Don Riggio has blended his never ending factual pearls about my favorite music genre and sprinkled them throughout his beautifully crafted sequel, *Beyond Vinyl*. We are once again swept into the world of the Du-Kanes as they sing their way through a musical journey filled with twists and turns. "Bravo Don.""

Mike Miller - Harmony Street ™

Dedication

Over the past several years it has been my distinct honor and pleasure to meet and talk with a great many of the artists, executives and media personalities whose music has given me so much pleasure. I now consider many of them close friends. Their stories and experiences made the technical portions of my books much easier to write. I thank them all and dedicate this book to them.

To my wife Carol, whose become an "author's widow," while I toil away doing research, writing and marketing my work. I love you sweetheart.

Acknowledgements

Writing can indeed be a solitary endeavor. I consider myself fortunate to have the resources of the Henderson Writers Group here in Las Vegas to help me along. Our weekly critique meetings offer great advice and the opportunity for camaraderie within the writing community. To all who've offered advice on my novels, I thank you. Three of you in particular made invaluable contributions to the work contained within these pages:

Lyn Robertson – Editor: Though we quibbled over apostrophes and past pronouns, the finished product exemplifies her talent and ability to create a work any author can be proud of.

Lyn can be reached at: **linktolyn@gmail.com**

Michael O'Neal – Cover Design: Once again his vision of my cover concept was right on and portrayed all the elements necessary to attract readers to the work.

Michael can be reached at: **devilsplayground@live.com**

Martin Greening – E-Book Expert: His superior grasp of the world of internet publishing has put my work on a new and wonderful plateau.

Martin can be reached at: **martin@aryus.com**

About the Author

Beyond Vinyl is the second installment of Donald Riggio's rock and roll trilogy. The first book, *Seven-Inch Vinyl*, became a #1 Kindle Best Seller. It chronicles the early days of rock and roll, between the years 1953 and 1969. *Beyond Vinyl* continues the narrative into the baby boomer years through to the inception of the Rock and Roll Hall of Fame. The final installment, *When Gold Turns to Gray*, is scheduled for publication late in 2013 and will move the oldies genre into the new millennium as fans endeavor to "keep the music alive."

Mr. Riggio enjoys great success with his Donald Riggio Facebook page. His nearly four thousand friends post and discuss old time rock and roll news, pictures and music links 24/7. He invites all to join and post often. His blog: **seven-inch-vinyl.blogspot.com** keeps fans and readers up-to-date on the progress and success of his novels.

He lives in Las Vegas, Nevada with his wife Carol and their cocker spaniel puppy, Brandi.

"We may be finished with the past,

but the past is not finished with us."

-Dr. Bergen Evans

Prologue:
"The Waldorf"

January 23, 1986

A pretty blonde in her early twenties stood at the curb outside Ecclisse, the trendy eatery in New York City's Little Italy district. She raised her hand in an attempt to snare a passing vacant taxicab. The restaurant enjoyed a renewed popularity owing to the number of celebrities now frequenting the place. Jackie Kennedy Onassis and Henry Kissinger were regulars. The constant presence of music industry types like Madonna, Lionel Richie, and newcomer Whitney Houston ensured an ample number of paparazzi would gather outside, even now during the lunch hour.

She wore a brown leather bomber jacket, tight blue jeans and cowboy boots, appropriate for this drizzly winter day. A sudden gust of wind tangled her long hair in a green scarf she had wrapped around her neck. A large leather purse hung from her shoulder by a strap.

Her efforts soon paid off as a yellow cab maneuvered its way across a lane of traffic and came to a stop in front of her.

"The Waldorf, side entrance please," she said with resolve after getting in and closing the door behind her.

The driver threw the flag on the meter and merged into traffic. Years of experience had him plot out the route in his head. The Waldorf Astoria Hotel was on Park Avenue between 49th and 50th Streets. The lights along Broadway would be against him at this time of day and the drive crosstown guaranteed a good fare.

He squared his passenger's reflection in his rear-view mirror as the girl settled in for the ride. She removed her scarf and shook out her hair. She was pretty and nicely made up, but if she was a celebrity *he* didn't recognize her. An old Neil Sedaka song played through the speaker of the transistor radio wedged on his dashboard. The girl hummed along. He was surprised she knew the song.

Her specific instruction to take her to the side entrance proved to be the right idea. Traffic in front of the hotel was snarled and barely moving. Horns blared. Obviously some major event was taking place later that evening.

When the cab turned the corner the girl leaned forward in her seat. "You can drop me off anywhere around here."

"This is just the side entrance Miss," he responded.

"That's fine." When the vehicle stopped next to a parked car she handed the driver a fifty dollar bill.

"Aw sweetheart," he complained mildly, "I can't break this."

"You can keep the change."

She hopped out of the taxi and scurried along the sidewalk to knock on a door of the art deco building. A sign on the door read: DELIVERY ENTRANCE. The door soon opened from the inside and the girl reached for her wallet again.

The driver's attention was diverted by the tapping of an object on his rear fender. He looked to see a tall policeman in his winter blues waving his nightstick.

"C'mon pal, move it," the cop ordered.

"Yeah, yeah, I'm goin."

Before hitting the gas, he looked again to his right. The girl was gone. The delivery door closed. He wondered, *pretty girl, fancy restaurant, delivery entrance, throwing money around*?

"Man," he said out loud, "I hope she ain't no hooker."

♫♫♫♫♫

Inside, the girl showed her room key to the Hispanic maintenance worker who let her into the hotel. She tipped him and then hurried along a deserted corridor until she reached a bank of service elevators. She took one to the tenth floor. After exiting the car, she continued on at a more leisurely pace along the richly carpeted hallway to room 1013. She unlocked the door as quietly as she could. Once inside she removed her jacket and tossed it and her scarf onto the sofa in the center of the main area of the posh suite. The girl made her way along the wall leading to the two bedrooms the suite featured. She peeked into one of the bedrooms and what she saw made her smile.

A man sat in an easy chair placed before a large window overlooking the street. His back was to her. She tiptoed along until she was close enough to pounce out at him.

"Boo!" she shouted.

Joseph Rabinowitz was startled. "Goodness Danielle, you coulda given me a heart attack."

The girl came around in front of him and hugged him tightly. She kissed him on the cheek before flittering off toward the king-size bed where she belly-flopped right into the middle of the mattress.

The years had been good to Joseph. Like his late father Solomon, he sported a full head of silver gray hair. His featured a thin yet decidedly darker streak that ran part way through which, as Danielle put it, gave him "a pervy look." At fifty-one he kept himself in good shape. Still, at times his lower back ached with arthritis, the result of a car accident he suffered in his army days. Severe nearsightedness also required he now wear eyeglasses full-time.

"Where's your mother?" he asked.

"I ditched her." Danielle rolled onto her back. She bent one leg at the knee and crossed her other leg over it.

"You did what?"

"Yeah. We came out of Bergdorf's and she wanted to keep shopping. I wanted to have lunch at Ecclisse. She didn't want to go there, so first chance I got, I ditched her."

Joseph shook his head. "She's gonna be miffed."

Danielle simply shrugged.

Their conversation was interrupted by the sound of the hotel room door opening and the rustling of paper shopping bags. A stern voice called out, "Danielle! Come out here please."

"Uh-oh," Danielle uttered softly, "she saw my jacket."

"Better go face the music."

"Do I have to?"

"Go."

She leapt from the bed and hopped across the room. She again kissed Joseph, this time on the top of his head. "I love you Daddy," she said before skipping off.

Daddy. The word still sounded good to him. Danielle was not his biological daughter. He adopted her fifteen years ago, soon after he and his wife Janet remarried.

Joseph heard raised voices from the other room but couldn't make out any details of the conversation. Janet entered the bedroom and tossed three department store shopping bags on the bed.

Now in her forties, she was still stunning to look at. When she and Danielle shopped together, people might easily mistake them for sisters. Right now though, she wasn't happy with her daughter. "I'm going to brain that kid one of these days. Did she tell you what she did?"

Joseph stood and moved to the opposite side of the bed to help her with her loot.

"She told me she ditched you because you didn't want to go to lunch at Ecclisse."

"That's right," she said as she folded a new sweater.

"You *used* to like that place a lot."

"That was a long time ago. I don't like what it's become now. All those reporters and photographers milling around trying to drudge up vile gossip… Anyway, I think she gave me the slip so she could go meet someone."

Joseph knew whom she meant. "She should know better."

"Well apparently she doesn't care." Janet changed the subject, "and what about you? Why are you still just sitting here looking out that window?" It was his turn to be scolded.

"Just reminiscing."

"Well, I'll tell you what I told our daughter. We need to be dressed and ready for dinner by six. We have a big night ahead. It won't do for any of us to be late. Shall I shower first?"

"Yes, go ahead."

After she left the room, Joseph returned to the easy chair. He paused for a moment to look down into the street. He missed the city. Since the seventies they'd been living in a large home in the very upscale Westchester County town of Rye. The sights and sounds of Manhattan always made him think of the old days.

Janet was right, this would be a very special night indeed. Now, as he sat and rested his head against the soft upholstery, he closed his eyes and welcomed the memories of another big night many years ago.

Chapter One:
"Reunion-Revisited"

October 18th 1969

The din of a dozen conversations resonated throughout the backstage area of the Majestic Theater in mid-town Manhattan. It was nearly midnight. Moments earlier the venue played host to "An Evening of Solid Gold," a sold-out rock and roll reunion concert. The show featured an array of performers who recorded for Chanticleer Records, one of the most successful independent record labels of the fifties and early sixties.

It was a re-birth of sorts for Joseph Rabinowitz, the thirty-four year old entrepreneur and co-founder of the label. His life had been in shambles for the past five years. An idyllic marriage ended in divorce. The music empire he created with his business partner Leo Klein came crashing down around his ears. The onslaught of the British music invasion very nearly destroyed the American music industry.

The success of this show gave Joseph a sense of vindication. It provided a rare happy moment in his professional life that now spilled backstage. Still, more personal disappointments tempered his enthusiasm.

Then, in what seemed like the very next instant…

"Hey, look who I found wandering around!" The voice of Curtis Tinnsley, the show's music director, somehow managed to gain the attention of several of those gathered, Joseph among them.

Curtis led Joseph's ex-wife, Janet, by the arm into the backstage area. Excusing himself from a conversation with a reporter, Joseph made his way across the crowded space. Janet smiled and lowered her head as he drew near.

"You know this woman Joe?" Curtis asked.

"She looks vaguely familiar," he joked taking both of her hands in his. He resisted the temptation to kiss her.

"It was nice seeing you again Janet," Curtis said.

"Same here Curtis," she replied as he walked off.

Weeks before, she surprised Joseph by showing up at his apartment with her five year old daughter. It was the first time the couple had seen one another since Janet moved to London shortly after their divorce. Her daughter Danielle came about as a result of the love affair she had with a British rock star named Ian Markham. Although Joseph invited Janet to the concert at that time, she told him she wouldn't be able to attend. Now, he felt more than happy to see her.

"Why didn't you call me? I would have sent tickets."

"It was a last minute thing. There was a change of plans, so here I am."

"You're alone?"

"Yes I am."

"My, my," a voice said from behind them. They turned to see Leo Klein approaching. His was another familiar face from her younger days. "Joseph told me you'd been in town, but he didn't expect you to show up."

"It was a last minute thing," she repeated. Janet tilted her head to accept his gracious kiss to her cheek.

Leo looked to Joseph. "We should wrap things up here."

"Yes," Joseph replied before telling Janet, "we're having a party at Monahan's on Sixth. You'll join us?"

"Oh, I think not. I just wanted to come back and congratulate everyone."

"Nonsense," Leo said.

"Leo's right, you're coming," he thought for a moment before adding, "unless…where's Danielle?"

"With her nanny, she's fine."

"Then it's settled. You can ride with us. I'll get this crowd started. Leo will you take Janet and get us a cab?"

"Certainly," Leo smiled as he took her by the arm.

♫ ♫ ♫ ♫ ♫

Monahan's Irish Pub was a chain of taverns situated throughout New York City. Their location on 59th Street featured a large downstairs banquet room seating close to one hundred people. It had a low wood beamed ceiling, rich oak paneling and soft muted lighting. More than a dozen long tables were set up side-by-side. The room filled to near capacity by the time everyone arrived. Many who knew Janet from the old days monopolized her time swapping stories and catching up. Among them, Johnny Seracino and Bobby Vitale from the label's most successful male singing group, the Du-Kanes. She chatted with the two remaining original members of the girl group the Pixies, Althea Rhodes and Roberta Johnson. In her songwriting days with Joseph she wrote many hit songs for them and others.

She also enjoyed a long conversation with Mickey Christie, an old friend and Joseph's sound engineer. Mickey's wife Linda had been her closest friend and confidant. Now they lived on the West Coast with two children of their own. They had fun looking at snapshots of their kids.

Joseph also found himself occupied with other matters, business matters.

"People are going to be talking about tonight's show for a long time," Jacob Miliewski offered in a soft voice. The well-known New York disc jockey was the evening's Master of Ceremonies. He sat with Joseph and Leo at a smaller table off to one side of the room.

"Jacob's right," Leo said. "This was beyond our wildest dreams."

"Listen kid," Miliewski told Joseph, "you gotta strike while the iron is hot. First thing tomorrow morning, you start making plans for the next one."

"Next one?" Joseph asked with surprise. "Jacob this was a one shot deal."

"Sure, sure, when we thought it was a risk that's the only way you *could* look at it. But we beat the odds...proved it could work. If *you* don't follow up on it you can bet your ass somebody *else* will."

Leo's eyes widened at the thought of yet another money making opportunity.

"Joseph, we should at least discuss it."

"Okay," Joseph relented, "but not tonight. Let's sleep on it."

"That's the ticket," Jacob beamed.

As the festivities wound down, many partygoers headed home. Joseph and Janet finally had time to sit together and enjoy a quiet conversation.

She told him of her relationship problems with Ian Markham, drug related incidents which had been made public. "I'm not returning to England," she explained taking Joseph by surprise. "I won't expose Dani to all that."

"How do you think Ian will react?"

"He'll be angry...hurt. He does love his daughter very much. He just doesn't have a place in his life for us anymore." Joseph looked away. "Sorry," Janet added realizing she once said the exact same thing about *him*. "I don't think I'll have an easy time of it."

"Janet, I want you to understand that you won't have to go through this alone."

She managed a smile and a single thought entered her mind, ice cream.

🎵🎵🎵🎵🎵

The first thing Janet *saw* when she opened her eyes the next morning were two empty one-pint ice cream cartons on the nightstand. Sometime, while living abroad, she acquired a taste for strawberry ice cream over butter pecan. Rather than quibble about it, they bought a pint of each.

The first thing she *heard* was the deep breathing of Joseph asleep beside her. He looked peaceful, a combination of relief from the nervous tension of the concert and satisfaction from their session of fiery lovemaking.

The decision to go back to the apartment with him was impulsive, to be sure. Caught up in the exhilaration of the events, she couldn't refuse his invitation. In this afterglow moment she felt no regrets. Joseph still loved her. She knew this from the first time she visited him with Danielle weeks before. As to her own feelings, she wasn't sure.

Joseph woke and slid over to face her. She responded by lying flat on her back. He reached his arm across her belly. "Should I make us breakfast?"

"Goodness, Joseph it *must* be lunch time by now."

"Alright then, lunch."

"I really should be getting back. I don't often leave Dani with her nanny overnight."

"Can I call you later…dinner?"

"Not tonight," then, before he could protest, "tomorrow perhaps… We'll have time for all this Joseph, I promise."

"I need a shower and caffeine."

"Go ahead. I'll make coffee."

He kissed her on the cheek before getting out of bed.

She laid there listening to the shower run and thought about what she told him. Was *she* ready or even willing to renew the relationship she fled just a few years before?

She left the bed and walked to the closet. There she found several neatly pressed white dress shirts hanging in a row. She put one on, buttoned a single button across her breasts and started toward the kitchen.

Once the coffee was on, she took the time to look around the apartment. Last time she noticed a new addition to the furnishings, a bookcase standing some eight feet high in the middle of one wall of the living room. As she approached to inspect its contents, she wondered how he ever found the time to read. She scanned a row of titles and found them, standing spine to spine, the four photo books she published abroad. The first two contained pictures from the English and

Scottish countryside. The third featured photos from Germany and the fourth from the Netherlands, both done while she toured with Ian's band the Have Knots. She reached up and ran her fingers along the spines of the books. Seeing her work on his bookshelf gave her a warm happy feeling.

Joseph was fully dressed as he entered the living room. "Coffee smells good."

"Should be just about done."

"Better hurry if you wanna shower before all the hot water is gone."

"Interesting collection you have here."

"For show mostly. I never seem to have any time to read these days."

Janet smiled.

Chapter Two:
"Geep"

"Are you sure it's okay for him to stay?" Jeannie Liebermann asked her friend Barbara Seracino. "I can go down, wake him up and drag his ass home." Jeannie was married to Kenny Liebermann, the third original member of the Du-Kanes.

"It's fine. I'll make all three of them breakfast in the morning before I send Kenny home," Barbara assured her.

The Seracinos, Liebermanns and Bobby Vitale left the party at Monahan's early, because Bobby was scheduled to fly back to his home in Las Vegas the next afternoon. On the drive from the city, adrenalin still pumped through the veins of the singers. They decided to stop at the Seracino house for a nightcap.

Johnny grabbed a bottle of Grappa, a strong grape based Italian brandy, from a cabinet in the dining room. He led his friends downstairs to the basement. Barbara put up a pot of coffee for her and Jeannie. A short time later, the harmonic tones of male voices emanated from below. It lasted for about an hour. After things went quiet, Jeannie went and took a peek.

"The three of them are sound asleep," she reported to Barbara with a chuckle.

"Leave them right where they are."

"Okay then. I'll call you tomorrow." Jeannie picked up her purse and Barbara walked her to the door. "It was quite a night for our guys, huh? All of us really."

"Yeah, it *was* fun."

"I don't know about you, but I felt like we were back in the old days when we were all kids again."

They hugged at the front door as Jeannie left.

Barbara closed up the house, changed into a nightgown and went to bed. She wasn't used to the empty space beside her and couldn't fall asleep. She thought about what Jeannie said. Her mind filtered all the way back to 1958, the year they *stopped* being kids.

🎵🎵🎵🎵🎵

Johnny and Barbara hurried up the ramp from the basement of their building in the Throggs Neck Project. It was late. They'd been in the carriage room making love. Johnny had an extra key to the basement made so Barbara wouldn't have to keep snatching the one from her mother's pocket book. They managed to stash away two pillows, a couple of towels and a top sheet into a duffel bag Barbara found in her parent's apartment. The linens made their trysts more comfortable. Since doing the laundry was one of Barbara's household chores, she was able to clean them regularly. Playing house became very easy. They giggled as they reached the top of the ramp. There they ran headlong into another neighborhood boy, someone they both knew.

"Jesus Geep," Johnny yelled, "you scared us half to death man!"

"Sorry Johnny," the other boy said sheepishly.

"Johnny don't call him by that terrible name," Barbara said. Neighborhood kids slapped the insulting nickname "Geep" onto Jimmy Stannic, the boy who lived with his family in apartment 3A of their building.

"Yeah, okay, I'm sorry," Johnny said. "You been standing here long?"

"Naw, I just snuck out for a smoke. What were you guys doing down there?"

Johnny was quick to answer. "Oh...uh...we were just putting some stuff in the carriage room for Barbara's mom."

"It's pretty spooky down there, ain't it?"

"Yeah," Barbara answered shyly, "kinda."

Johnny wrapped things up. "Well, I'm gonna walk Barbara upstairs. See ya."

"Night Jimmy," Barbara said with a smile.

"Goodnight Barbara," Jimmy replied.

The couple went up to the second floor landing and stood outside the door to the Borelli apartment. Running into Jimmy sidetracked Barbara. She had put off telling Johnny something very important. But if she told him now, she feared he might get mad and start shouting. That might draw the attention of her parents inside.

"Can we stop at the candy store after school tomorrow and talk, just you and me?" Barbara asked.

"You know I have rehearsal tomorrow. We gotta get ready for the Aquinas dance on Saturday."

"Please Johnny, it's important."

"If it's so important, tell me now."

"No, it's okay. It can wait."

Her took her in his arms and kissed her hard. "After practice we'll talk. I promise."

He let go of her and bolted downstairs. Barbara quietly opened the apartment door and slipped inside, disappointed that she hadn't told him that her period was two weeks late.

Down in the lobby, Jimmy Stannic hid in a corner near the mailboxes where he wouldn't be seen. He had tiptoed inside right after Johnny and Barbara headed upstairs. Jimmy listened carefully but all he could make out was hushed conversation. He had become adept at spying on his neighbors. All three of their bedroom windows lined up directly above one another. Johnny's room on the first floor, Barbara's on the second with Jimmy's on the third and top floor.

Some evenings the two lovers chatted with one another through their open windows, unaware that Jimmy listened from just a few feet above. If they talked about sex, Jimmy often played with himself afterward. He wasn't as stupid as other people thought. He knew the two of them were screwing in the basement. Just because he didn't get good marks in school and didn't like to read, the other kids thought he was dumb. That's why they gave him that stupid nickname

"Geep."

Nobody even seemed to know what the name meant. Barbara told him that she once read about something called a "geek show" where a guy in a carnival act bit the head off live chickens. Jimmy didn't think it applied to him because people called him "Geep" and not "geek." Besides, he never bit the head off a live chicken. Barbara said the nickname was mean and cruel and didn't use it. Jimmy liked it when she told Johnny earlier not to call him Geep either.

He liked Johnny and enjoyed listening to his group the Du-Kanes. He wished they would make it big someday. But he wished it for a different reason than everyone else. Jimmy's younger sister, Joanie was part of Barbara's crowd. She told him that Barbara sometimes talked about being jealous of other girls who fawned over Johnny's singing. She worried he might be tempted to cheat on her.

Jimmy thought that if Johnny became successful he might break up with her and move away from the neighborhood. Then maybe *he* could ask her out and be her boyfriend. Then she'd screw him in the basement instead.

Jimmy liked Barbara. He liked Barbara a lot.

A couple of weeks later, Barbara dropped out of school. No one knew why. It didn't matter though, Jimmy was going to quit school too. He failed many of his subjects and would have to repeat a year. That embarrassed and angered his parents.

His father got him a job as a track maintenance worker with the New York City Transit Authority. Now he would have a good paying job with benefits. All the other guys would be impressed to see him leaving the court every morning with a big gunmetal gray lunch box, just like his dad.

However, from the very first day, his job proved to be more than a bit frightening. The subway tunnels were dark and smelled of urine and garbage. Huge rats and bugs were everywhere.

"Listen to me Jimmy, and listen good," Frank Stannic shined the beam of his flashlight on the train tracks below their feet. He was about to teach his son an important lesson. "Those two side-by-side rails there; them are just ordinary running rails. They're harmless. But, see that other rail just next to them, the one covered with wood? That's called the third rail, the conductor rail. It carries twelve hundred volts of direct electrical current through it. That current is what makes the trains run." He leaned in closer to his son, put his large hands on the boy's shoulders and looked him deeply in the eyes. "Jimmy, if you touch that third rail you'll fry like an egg. I'm serious. I seen it happen and it ain't pretty." Pointing an index finger in the boy's face, he repeated his stern warning. "Remember, if you touch it you die…You die!"

♫♫♫♫♫

Johnny dropped Kenny off at his home on their way to bring Bobby to Kennedy Airport for his flight home. A good breakfast and several cups of Barbara's strong coffee helped deaden the after effects of the Grappa the men drank the night before. Johnny and Bobby still buzzed about the show.

"I'm telling you Johnny," Bobby said, "I heard plain as day, Miliewski telling Joe Rabin and Leo Klein that they should plan on doing more shows. They all must have made a fortune."

Bobby's reference to Joe "Rabin" stemmed from the fact that years ago, Joseph found his name shortened by Jacob Miliewski in an radio interview.

"Maybe so Bobby. Doing more shows would really be nice. But how would you work that out? I mean, do you plan to take time off and fly back and forth from Vegas? That's crazy man."

"No, fuck that. No more dealing blackjack for me. Being onstage again got my blood boiling. Tomorrow I'm putting an ad in the local papers looking for some singers. I'm gonna get a vocal group together. Maybe call it Bobby Vitale's Du-Kanes. Do all of our old tunes."

Johnny glanced his way with some concern. "Joe Rabin might not like that."

"I don't give a shit what he likes. I'll be three thousand miles away in Vegas. What's he gonna do sue me?"

Chapter Three:
"Starting Over"

Joseph basked in the limelight of the reunion concert. Critics and music industry people heaped accolades and praise upon his efforts. *Billboard* magazine reported:

> "With this show, Rabinowitz has rekindled a flame that's dwindled since the arrival of the Beatles."

Cash Box magazine had a similar review:

> "A great night of oldies. We hope it starts a trend that continues for a long time."

Joseph made a concerted effort to inject himself back into the lives of his former wife and her daughter. It was his second chance to re-connect with Janet and make amends for the mistakes he made causing her to leave in the first place. Now he had the opportunity to fulfill the dream they both had in happier days, to raise a family.

Janet and Danielle lived in the hotel suite she rented by the month. The three of them shared dinner twice a week. For Halloween they went trick or treating in the apartment building with Danielle dressed as a pirate. When Thanksgiving rolled around Janet insisted on making dinner. They watched the *Macy's Thanksgiving Day Parade* on television and enjoyed a great meal. While Danielle napped, Janet and Joseph chatted over coffee. He told her of a meeting he had earlier in the week with Jacob Miliewski. The disc jockey still pressed Joseph to commit to more reunion shows.

"He's not letting up at all. He's even got Leo in on the act. I got three calls from him in Florida already."

"Are you so opposed to doing it?" Janet asked.

Joseph thought for a moment before answering. "My

priorities are different now."

"Would it be fair to say that I may have something to do with that?"

"I let the music business come between us once before. I'm not going to let that happen again."

"I'd like to think that we're both older and wiser than we were back then." Janet paused before explaining further, "I wouldn't want the fact that I'm back in your life to influence a decision as important as this one. Danielle and I aren't going anywhere. But I do agree that if *you* don't do more shows someone *else* will."

In December, they expanded their visit to Rockefeller Center to include a performance of the giant stage show at Radio City Music Hall. Afterward they moved on to view the Christmas tree lighting. It was a wonderful moment. They reveled in the awe Danielle displayed as she took in the sights and sounds around her. Janet held the child in her arms so she could see above the heads of those in front of them. When the switch was thrown illuminating the towering spruce, Danielle let out a gasp of excitement. Janet swallowed the lump of emotion in her throat. She leaned back into Joseph seeking his solid strength to bolster her.

They lingered until the crowd thinned a bit allowing them to move closer to the railing separating the spectators from the tree. Janet put Danielle down for her to peer through the railing.

"I have something for you," Joseph's voice from behind made her turn to face him. He offered her a small gift wrapped box.

"I wasn't aware we were exchanging gifts."

"This is something special."

Their words caught Danielle's attention. "Open it Mommy."

Janet unwrapped and opened the gift, feeling sure as to what she'd find inside. It was a large marquis-cut diamond ring. She did not look at him when she spoke. "This wasn't necessary. I still have the last ring you gave me."

"I know. I just figured that the second time around it should be bigger."

"It's so pretty. Isn't it?" the child beamed.

"Yes it is Dani. It's truly beautiful."

"Put it on," she urged with a smile.

Janet did so and held out her hand for her to see.

"Oooo, will you wear it Mommy?"

Janet looked Joseph in the eyes. "Yes, I will."

There hadn't been much in the way of a Christmas celebration in the Rabinowitz apartment in the five years Janet had been away. That was about to change. They shopped for a tree from a lot on the corner of 90th Street and Broadway. It took time for Danielle to give her seal of approval to an eight-foot spruce with branches that extended full and wide. Though they found several dusty boxes of decorations in the basement, Janet insisted on buying others during a 5th Avenue shopping spree. Christmas Day proved festive; wrapping paper was knee high by the time Danielle was through opening her gifts. As always, Janet took lots of pictures.

The three of them huddled together on the sofa on New Year's Eve to watch the lighted "time ball" drop 77 feet down a pole atop One Times Square, a 25-story skyscraper on the corner of 42nd Street and Broadway. Danielle fell asleep long before the countdown to midnight. Joseph and Janet sipped a champagne toast from plastic glasses. They had truly endured much and spent half the decade apart. Now they were together again, ready for a new decade…a new beginning.

♫♫♫♫♫

Joseph and Janet re-married with little fanfare in January 1970. Leo Klein flew up from Florida alone. His wife, Gloria, didn't want any part of a trip to New York in the middle of winter. Jacob Miliewski also attended, as did the members of the Du-Kanes, the Pixies and their families. In lieu of a honeymoon, Joseph spent the following day in a meeting with Leo, Jacob and the Richards brothers from the Majestic Theater. They made plans for two shows in 1970, one in July and the other in November. All parties agreed that based on the success of these shows, the concerts might become annual events.

In a separate agreement, Joseph and Leo became partners once again. They called their new venture Chanticleer Enterprises. For now, the company would concentrate on producing the concerts, but the door was left open for future endeavors in the music and entertainment industries.

When word got out that Joseph and Leo were back in the music business, it pleased a good many people and angered others.

♫ ♫ ♫ ♫ ♫

"Fucking Jew bastard Joe Rabin. I told you we shoulda put two bullets behind his ear a long time ago." Phil Gambetta said angrily during a lunch meeting in Little Italy with his long-time business partner, Richie Conforti. The place was crowded with customers and Richie worried Phil's comment might be overheard.

"*Statti ziti,*" his admonition in Italian told Phil to shut his mouth. Richie had always been the brains of their operation. He brought the idea of getting into the record business to mob boss Don Guglielmo Viola. With their financing, their independent record company, Alexis Records was sure to succeed. They provided the stiffest competition to Joseph's legitimate endeavor throughout the sixties. Alexis' dirty dealings and unscrupulous methods helped them survive the British invasion while Joseph went under. "This news merely shows us that there may still be some things we can learn from Mr. *Rab-in-o-witz*." The way he drew out the syllables of Joseph's last name indicated that he did not totally disagree with Phil's assessment of the situation.

Further discussion would have to wait. A waiter brought out their appetizer, a double portion of Spedini alla Romana. A generous helping of mozzarella cheese baked inside a loaf of seasoned bread crumbs and topped with a zesty anchovy paste held their attention for the next half hour.

♪♪♪♪♪

In Joseph's mind, one order of business remained before embarking on the task of planning the next concert, Danielle's adoption. Janet didn't push the issue, but felt it wonderful that he insisted on it. She knew Ian Markham wouldn't take kindly to the idea that his only child would be living on another continent. Because Danielle didn't have Markham's name, he rarely publically admitted to being her father. After he was served with the legal papers in London, he did however counter-sue for custody.

Janet viewed this as a ploy on his part. It was common knowledge that his situation in Great Britain was tenuous to say the least. He'd been found guilty on criminal charges for selling drugs. His passport was confiscated and he faced a stiff jail term. No one wanted an ugly court battle playing out on both sides of the Atlantic involving drugs, a rock star and a young child.

Joseph's lawyers retained a top barrister in London. A deal was hashed out with the British High Court to keep Markham out of jail. In return, he dropped his custody case.

Six months later, Ian Markham was found dead of a drug overdose in a hotel room in Berlin. The news upset Danielle very much. To get everyone's mind off this tragedy, Joseph took Janet and Danielle to Florida for two weeks to visit his mother Myra. It was a wonderful time for them all.

Chapter Four:
"London"

When Janet arrived in London in February 1964, it was the second time in her life that new surroundings overwhelmed her. The first came a decade earlier when she left her home in Ohio to live with Joseph in New York City. Now she faced this drastic new change alone.

Once a drab black and white city, the burgeoning British music scene transformed London into an Oz-like wonderland. Businessmen in their black bowler hats shared the busy sidewalks with those splashed in the bright pastel colors of the latest in Carnaby Street fashion.

The youth of Great Britain was divided into two conflicting subcultures, the Mods and the Rockers. Mods dressed in the latest Italian suits and leather shoes. Women wore men's shirts and trousers or miniskirts with little make-up and short hair. They traveled on motor scooters and their musical tastes leaned toward American R&B and contemporary British acts like the Small Faces and the Who.

In stark contrast were the Rockers, an edgy biker group easily recognizable by their stripped down modified racing motorcycles. Their attire consisted of leather jackets, T-shirts and Levi jeans. They listened to 50's rock and roll stars like Eddie Cochran and Gene Vincent.

Oxford Street was a narrow cobblestone road typical of many off the Strand, a major London thoroughfare. Bright red double-decker buses jammed traffic in much the same way yellow cabs did in Manhattan. Homes on the street were called mews houses with large livery type doors at street level. Back in a time when the main mode of transportation was by horse-drawn Hansom cabs and carriages, the vehicles were stored and the animals stabled there. The drivers and their families lived in the lofts above.

In more recent years, the mews houses had been

renovated into finished apartments, quaint shops and coffee houses. Janet rented one such second floor loft suitable to her needs. At a nearby camera shop, she outfitted herself with all the equipment necessary to embark on her quest. Since childhood, Janet held an affinity for castles. Now she wanted to photograph medieval ruins, castles, and abbeys and publish them in a coffee table book. All she needed now was some way to get around.

Her landlord suggested she put up an advertisement in some of the local pubs, which might attract the attention of some university student eager to earn some extra cash. Two days later, she got a call about the ad from someone named Ian. They arranged to meet at a pub around the corner from her loft.

Janet sat a table sipping a glass of wine when the young man arrived.

"Miss Rabinowitz?" he asked.

Janet used her full last name in the hope no one in London would recognize it.

"Yes?" She looked up to see a tall and slender young man standing across the table from her. He looked to be about twenty. Long scraggily brown hair cascaded down to his shoulders. His face bore a dark five-o'clock shadow. He wore tight blue jeans flared at the bottom and a sweatshirt emblazoned with a logo of what she took to be a local sports team.

"Hello, I'm Ian, we spoke on the blower?" He motioned to the empty chair in front of him. "May I?"

She smiled and nodded her approval. Once seated, a waitress approached them.

"I'll have a pint of Guinness luv," he said.

After the waitress left the boy took the initiative. "Your ad said you've need of a driver?"

"Yes," Janet explained, "you see I'm planning on putting together a photo book on castles and other historical places. But I don't want to photograph all the tourist stuff that's already been done to death." She reached into her purse and produced several brochures that she pushed across the table. As he examined them she asked, "Do you know these places?"

A smile crossed his face. "Oh yes, ma'am. I surely do. But if you don't mind my sayin so, if they are in them brochures, well, that's the same touristy stuff yer lookin to avoid. I *do* know of some ruins and the like what ain't been photographed much as I can recall."

The waitress returned setting a beer in front of him.

"That's just the sort of thing I'm looking for. Are they nearby?" Janet asked as the young man downed half his drink in one swig.

"Pretty near…an hour's drive, maybe two."

"And you'll take me?"

"It would be my pleasure," he replied.

"How much shall I pay you?"

"Just a few quid…and expenses for petrol and all. We can work it out later."

"When are you available? Do you have classes?"

"Me, classes?" He chuckled. Ian felt comfortable talking to this woman and spoke more casually. "No mum, I don't go to university. I'm what you call a free agent. I'll come round for you."

"Okay, shall we say tomorrow morning at nine? I'm on Oxford Street, number twenty-two."

"Make it ten and we have a deal." Again, his rakish smile flipped across the table between them.

"Alright then, ten."

"Lovely."

Janet found it difficult to maintain eye contact. She sensed he flirted with her and didn't care to play into that scenario. She looked upon this as a business arrangement only.

Once again, the waitress stood at their table. "Can I get the two of you anything else?"

"I don't think so," Janet replied.

When Ian reached into his pocket, Janet put her hand out in protest. "No, this is my treat."

Ian relaxed his pose. "Well, in that case, do you care if I stay and have another?"

The waitress rolled her eyes as if to say, *cheeky bugger*.

"Please, enjoy yourself," Janet answered. She counted out some coins and handed them to the waitress. "Will that cover it and a little something for you?"

"That'll be smashing Miss."

She looked to Ian. "See you in the morning then?"

"Be there with bells," he nodded.

As she walked off she felt his eyes on her. It made her stir. Joseph had been the only man in her life who ever really meant anything to her, anyone else were merely temptations. There was a flirtatious fantasy about Teddy Boyette so long ago, and more recently the folk singer Alan Thomas who pressed her at a time when she was most vulnerable. This handsome young Brit possessed an alluring quality that made her feel giddy and foolish.

♫ ♫ ♫ ♫ ♫

Markham was twenty-five minutes late arriving the next morning. Janet stood outside on the street when he pulled up in a green Morris Oxford four-door station wagon. He got out and came around to open the door for her.

"Sorry to be so tardy mum," he apologized, "had a snit of a time rollin out of the rack this mornin. Were you waitin long?"

"Since *ten*," Janet replied stiffly.

"Well better than since nine what?" he joked.

Janet didn't find it funny. She got in while Ian shoved her photography gear in the back seat. Janet noticed two guitar cases and pieces of a drum kit in the back cargo area. Ian closed the door and hopped around to get in behind the wheel. He pulled away from the curb without much caution.

They hadn't driven five blocks when Ian announced, "I was in such a state rushin to get out that I missed me vittles. Mind if we stop for some take away?"

"Take away?"

"Yeah, a bite of food to go. I know a good place for some fish and chips right near here."

Janet thought the term amusing. "Wasn't it George Bernard Shaw who wrote that the Americans and the English were two peoples separated by a common language?"

"Was it that bloke Shaw or Lennon-McCartney? Seems them lads write everything these days." Ian's comments made Janet laugh and broke a good deal of tension.

As she sat waiting outside the food shop, Janet turned on the car radio. A loud English pop tune blared from the speaker. She lowered the volume as Ian returned with their food.

Her introduction to the English food staple of fish and chips reminded her of the first time she ate a dirty water hot dog from a New York street vendor with Joseph. It was tasty yet quite different. This meal consisted of a piece of deep fried codfish, covered in batter and served over similarly fried slab-cut potatoes. The most disconcerting detail was the wrapping around the delicacy.

"Is this really newspaper?" Janet asked.

Ian spoke with a mouthful of food. "There's a piece of wax paper sandwiched in between for sanitary purposes." He motioned to the radio. "Do you fancy Cliff Richard?"

"He's pretty good," she answered without looking at him. "How about you, do you like American music?"

"It's all the bloody rage innit? Elvis, Chuck Berry, Roy Orbison."

"How about Teddy Boyette?"

"Sure bet. Top gear, that one. Pity he offed so soon."

"Are you in a band?" She motioned to the musical instruments stacked in the back.

"Isn't everyone?" They both laughed. "Me and a couple of mates pick up a few bob on weekends bangin on skins and beltin out chords. Nothin major."

"Are you a mod or a rocker?"

Ian laughed. "I suppose you could call us 'Mockers', straddlin the fence between both sets of blokes...not wanting to ruffle anyone's feathers, what."

They talked more about music as they drove. Janet said nothing about her involvement in the music business. Ian was more than happy to ramble on about what he and his mates were up to.

When they reached their destination, the ruins of an old abbey, Janet was truly fascinated. They trudged up a steep hill to where a stone tower reached high into the sky. As she placed her hand on the stone it was cold to the touch and she could almost sense the history of the place vibrating through her fingertips. Janet spent the entire afternoon exposing roll after roll of film from different angles and distances. On the drive back to the city, it was she who went on and on about the wonderful time she had. She hoped Ian had more ideas on where to go for their next jaunt.

♫♫♫♫♫

Over the next several weeks, Ian drove her from one locale to another marveling at her skill and enthusiasm. Sometimes as they listened to the radio, he would talk more about his band. Like the story about how his group got an unusual name.

"My old dad likes to lecture me, specially when he's in his cups from bein at the pub after work. He sat me down one time and he says to me, 'Ian, there's just two kinds of people in the world, the haves and the have nots. Us Markhams, we're the have nots lad and don't ever forget that.' Well that bit always stuck with me. So when it came to pickin a name for our lot, I come up with the Have Knots only using a 'k' instead of an 'n' sort of like the Beatles done by messin with the spelling."

Janet soon had Ian pose for pictures at some of the places they visited. *To gain perspective* was how she put it but the truth was she enjoyed taking his picture and it became silly shared fun. Sometimes they met for lunch or coffee to review the proofs after they were developed. It was on one such occasion that Ian made a suggestion.

"One of my mates, Andy, is from Yorkshire up north. There's a town there called Middlesbrough. He told me about this abandoned priory up that way. Pretty historic stuff…closed down for years now. I was thinking maybe you might want to drive up and have a look?"

"Yorkshire is rather far off, isn't it?" Janet asked.

Ian nodded. "It's a ways. Too far for a day jaunt, we'd need to bunk out somewhere. I'm sure they have nice accommodations."

He worried about being too forward as he awaited her response.

"We could make a real outing of it," Janet beamed at him. "I'll make some sandwiches and we can even stop along the way and have a picnic."

Ian was relieved. "That's right, a real outing, just like you said."

They solidified their plans and two days later embarked on their road trip.

Chapter Five:
"That Night in Middlesbrough"

The Morris Oxford handled the road well for both the stretches of highway driving and the snaking curves of the one lane road winding through North Yorkshire. They stopped for a picnic lunch of sandwiches, cheese and bottled beer along a bank of the River Tees before continuing on into Middlesbrough. The town had undergone a long process of re-development. During the war, the steel industry located in the town made it a frequent target for bombing by the Luftwaffe. Many of the early and mid-Victorian buildings had been destroyed or badly damaged. After they arrived, Janet looked for a place to rent rooms.

"I'm sorry Miss, but we only have one room available," the white-haired desk clerk at the small local hotel apologized. She looked at the couple over her wire-rimmed glasses. "It's the spring planting festival at the old Newham Grange Farm you see. Been in operation since the 1800s. If you'd come two days from now, you'd have had the entire place all to yourself."

"Is there anywhere else in town…?"

"I doubt it Miss…the festival. But, the room we *do* have has twin beds."

Janet thought for a moment before reaching into her purse for some cash. "Okay, I'll take it. Two nights please."

Several minutes later, Janet and Ian entered the small sparsely furnished room. The twin beds took up most of the space, along with a four-drawer dresser with a small mirror attached. The tiny bathroom was barely adequate, just a commode and sink. In order to bathe or shower, one needed to use the larger facilities at the end of the hall. Janet carried a small overnight bag and the leather shoulder bag containing her photo gear. Ian tossed his weathered backpack onto one of the beds.

"Well, this is going to be quite cozy, init?" he joked.

"It was either this or camping out under the stars," Janet answered.

"Equally romantic," his wisecrack brought a look of concern to Janet's face. Ian put both hands out in front of him in a defensive stance. "Not to worry luv, I promise to be on my best behavior."

♫ ♫ ♫ ♫ ♫

They set out early the next morning for the Priory just north of town. It turned out to be everything she hoped for. Much of the wooden roof had rotted away. Beams of sunlight broke through the remaining planks creating brilliant shadows and shapes. It reminded her of the "night lace" that streamed into her bedroom window when she was a child in Cleveland. She used both color and black and white film stock to painstakingly capture the exquisite images she viewed through her camera lens.

That evening, they sat at the bar of a local restaurant for quite some time waiting for a table…*the festival*. Janet had a glass of wine and Ian two pints of lager. They shared another bottle of wine with their dinner of shepherd's pie. Janet was excited and chirped on about the day's events. Ian hung on every word.

When they returned to their room, the door had barely closed behind them when Ian reached out and spun her around. She was stunned, but offered no resistance when he kissed her hard on the lips. He guided her toward one of the beds and steered her down. Ian peeled off his shirt and positioned himself beside her. Janet looked him deeply in the eyes and moved her head toward his to welcome his probing tongue. Ian unbuttoned her blouse and slipped it over her shoulders. He was confident and sure. Janet unhooked her bra and once her breasts were uncovered, Ian leaned forward to take one in his mouth. She gasped slightly at the pressure of his teeth.

"Easy," she whispered in his ear. He hesitated only to begin again a moment later. She wished he would take his time, but his unbridled passion was evident after he undressed. She allowed herself to succumb to him and be swept away.

He was more patient the second time. Neither of them felt any qualms of guilt the next day. They pushed the twin beds together for their second night.

Back in London, Janet had time to think about what happened. The difference in age was bothersome. She viewed the entire experience as a common occurrence given the open sexual attitude of the time. No commitments were expected or offered and the intimacy they shared continued.

🎵🎵🎵🎵🎵

The proofs from the Middlesbrough shoot were spectacular, exhibiting Janet's best work so far. She was so filled with confidence that she prepared a portfolio and brought them around to some local publishing companies. One of them, Burnham Publications, showed great interest. She negotiated a contract with a condition that allowed her to provide some short verse and captions to accompany the photos. She signed a contract and her book, *The Priory*, was scheduled for publication. Janet was thrilled. Ian suggested that a celebration was in order.

🎵🎵🎵🎵🎵

The Have Knots had a semi-regular gig at a pub in Kensington called the Pour House. It was a huge smoke-filled tavern. Patrons were loud and boisterous. They cackled with laughter as they drank, played darts and billiards. The noise level made it difficult to hear the five piece band trying their best to entertain them.

It seemed the perfect place to celebrate Janet's book deal and for her to meet the band. That was a detail she hadn't considered. As a couple, she would now become part of Ian's social circle made up predominantly of singers and musicians. Her first impression of the others was that they seemed like a normal group of young Brits having fun while dreaming of fame and stardom.

Besides Ian, the other strong personality within the group was lead guitar player Andy Pullam. He was a thin rugged looking boy with sharp features. The remaining three were very much alike. Bass player Reggie Ashe had flaming red hair that spun in long flowing strands down over his shoulders. His high falsetto vocal timbre was almost angelic. But when he spoke he had a severe stuttering problem. This impediment rendered him shy and withdrawn in social situations. Colin Murphy hailed from Dublin, Ireland and played rhythm guitar. The youngest member was Willie Thorn, a pimply-faced lad who communicated best seated behind a drum kit. He showed great dexterity with a pair of sticks pounding on drumheads and cymbals.

Like so many similar British bands, the emphasis of their sound focused on the instrumental presentation rather than the vocal. Aside from Ian's strong voice and Reggie's high tenor there was no harmony to speak of, but more a unison type singing. Otherwise they met the standard criteria; they were loud, sang on key and looked good on stage.

It might have been an ideal situation, except for the drugs.

The band rehearsed twice during the week and on most Saturdays at Andy's loft on Falmouth Street. The first time Janet sat in, she thought of how much of a bachelor pad it was. It was messy, sparsely furnished and nothing matched. The place also carried the lingering aroma of marijuana.

All five members of the band freely smoked the drug either in cigarette form or through a glass bong, a pipe consisting of a vertical tube connected to a bowl. During the course of the evening they also popped Benzedrine, and other amphetamines. On top of this, they also drank beer to intensify the rush.

Janet disliked feeling judgmental. She knew recreational drug use was often a staple for rock and roll performers, but it bothered her to see it in Ian. She told him that when he drove her home.

"It's not like we're shooting heroin or anything like that…" Ian defended himself and his friends. "…it was just some weed and a few bennies. Don't be so uptight luv. We're not a bunch of strung out junkies. We just need a little boost to keep the juices flowing so to speak."

In the weeks that followed they saw little of one another. Janet kept busy preparing her book while the band practiced with renewed intensity. The Have Knots adopted a hard edged bluesy sound similar to groups like the Rolling Stones and the Kinks, who now followed the Beatles and others to America.

Their job at the Pour House became a regular weekly gig. New fans jammed the place. This younger clientele paid closer attention to the music. The increase in business was not lost on the pub's owners. They closed down the dartboard and removed the billiard table to make way for dancing. The Pour House became Greater London's equivalent to the Cavern Club in Liverpool.

Though the band's popularity soared, Janet felt uncomfortable in the club scene. The girls that followed the group were, for the most part, giddy gum snapping teenagers that chain-smoked and pranced about in mini-skirts and tank tops. Despite their constant presence, she trusted Ian even though there *were* times when he'd show up at her flat drunk or stoned and smelling of cheap perfume.

♪ ♪ ♪ ♪ ♪

Janet agreed to attend a special party at the club on the weekend between Christmas and New Year's 1964. The event was cloaked in a bit of mystery with Ian promising some exciting news. Between the band's first and second set, it was Andy who stood and asked for quiet from the gathering of about a dozen close friends.

"As you all well know, we've been toiling away in this den of iniquity in the hope of being *discovered*. Well I'm happy to say that two nights ago, we were approached by a rep from Dunham Abbey Records and offered a contract..." A murmur of excitement, cheers and light applause rose from their party. As Andy relayed further details, Janet leaned in closer to Ian.

"Why didn't you say something?" she whispered.

"We wanted it to be a surprise. We're all abuzz," he whispered back. Then he kissed her.

Andy finished his announcement to exuberant offers of congratulations. Everyone was talking at once.

Reggie stammered, "N-n-now all we need is a g-g-great song for our first r-r-record." He then turned to Janet. "You c-c-could write us a hit record couldn't you Miss? Ian says you've written lots of them."

All the color drained from Janet's face. Ian and Andy looked at one another.

Almost as though she suddenly snapped out of a trance, Janet stood. "If you'll excuse me, I have to use the ladies room."

She walked away from the table. Ian was out of his chair and after her in an instant. He caught up with her in a corridor leading to the rest rooms.

"Wait Janet, let me explain." He grabbed her by the arm and turned her to face him.

"How long have you known who I was?" she asked in disbelief.

Ian shrugged, the beginning of an excuse formed in his

mind, but he thought better of it and admitted, "From the first really... first day I saw your ad. I recognized the name...made some inquiries."

"And all this time...you said *nothing?*" Her voiced cracked with emotion. "Just so you could get me to write songs for your shitty band?"

"No, no, it wasn't anything like that, Janet I..." He decided on a half truth this time. "Okay, maybe at first when I was driving you around, I thought I might get you to write a song for us. But after that night in Middlesbrough, everything changed. It was never supposed to come out like this, I swear. Please come back to the table."

Janet shook her head. "No, I can't. I have to go."

"But what should I tell the others?"

"Tell them...you know what Ian? I really don't give a shit *what* you tell them." Janet pulled away in tears and headed toward the ladies room. She barely made it to the commode before vomiting violently, which was becoming a common occurrence.

When Ian returned to the table, the demeanor of those seated had changed dramatically. "I oughtta stove your head in with a brick," he scolded Reggie.

"I'm sorry, Ian I d-d-didn't mean to blurt it out like that."

"Why couldn't you just keep your stuttering mouth shut?"

Andy spoke in defense of his band mate. "Don't beat yourself up about it Reg. Someone had to say something to her sooner or later. Lord knows if we left it up to dear sweet pussy-whipped Ian over here, we'd never have gotten a record out of her."

His admonition angered Ian. "Shut your hole, Andy. How much chance of anything like that happening now do you suppose there is? I told you I was working at my own pace."

"That's bullshit mate and you know it. What sense is it

to be having it on with a bird like that if you aren't going to make use of her? You came round months ago all warm and bubbly sayin how you latched on to this boffo American songwriting bimbo, and how you were going to weasel your way between the sheets and get her to write us some songs. Whatever happened to *that* grand plan, eh bucko?"

Ian had no answer.

His telephone calls to Janet the next day went unanswered. He waited another day before going to her flat.

"She went off early yesterday morning with all her gear," the landlord told him. "Said she'd be gone several days is all I know."

"But did she say *where* she was going?"

"No lad, she did not."

Ian was concerned and angry. His golden goose had flown away.

♫ ♫ ♫ ♫ ♫

It was a futile attempt at escape. A taxi brought her to a hotel close to her publisher's office on the opposite side of the city. Immersing herself by working on her book helped quell the anger and turmoil she felt at being used by Ian. This uncharacteristic emotional rollercoaster, and the topsy-turvy condition of her stomach, indicated something else was amiss.

When she returned to her flat she found all the apologetic notes Ian left for her under the door. She made an appointment to see a doctor. A few days later, she telephoned Ian and asked to meet him at the pub near her flat.

"I'm pregnant," she told him. Her stunning news reflected on his face. "I don't want to raise this child without a father Ian."

He forced a smile, reached across the table and took her hands in his. "No worries luv. I'm prepared to do the right thing. You'll see. Everything is going to be just fine. The people at the record company have got big plans for us. We're already setting up some recording sessions, and an album, and then a tour. They say maybe in two or three years we'll go to America."

She wanted to leap across the table and shake him. He took the news about becoming a father and swept it aside, concerned more about his band, making a record and being famous. Perhaps the decision she made to stay with him and raise their child together was a mistake. Then it occurred to her that perhaps *she* was the selfish one. Ian was a young man with a dream and on the threshold of success. Certainly having a baby with an older woman wasn't part of that equation.

♫♫♫♫♫

The Have Knots released their first single "Crossroads Encounter," an old R&B tune to which the band added a rollicking guitar driven performance. The song was a mild success on the British charts. Their follow up, another up-tempo rocker "Milltown Blues," crept into the top ten.

Ian asked Janet to accompany him to the offices of the record company for a meeting. She supposed it had something to do with the fact that she remained adamant about not writing any new songs for the band. She did make a concession to allow the Have Knots to use two songs on their first LP she and Joseph had written for the Du-Kanes in the early fifties, "Rye Beach Rock" and "When He's Around." However, Adrian McAuliffe the A&R man assigned to the band had something else on his mind.

"We anticipate big things for the band." McAuliffe was a stout older man in his forties with greasy hair and wore a rumpled suit. Janet didn't like him. "We're going to release one more single and then go back into the studio to record the rest of the album. Then the boys will go out on a six week local tour. I know you're well aware of how important image is for the success of something like this?" Janet was indeed aware of it and knew exactly where McAuliffe was headed. "We know you and Ian are expecting and we're all pleased about the blessed event. However, I'm sure you'll agree it would be better for everyone concerned if the female fans thought all the boys were single and *unencumbered* shall I say? A weasel-like smile crossed his face. "Believe me, we here at Dunham Abbey have only your best interests at heart."

Janet looked at Ian who sat silently like a scolded child in the principal's office leaving it for her to respond. She began quietly and calmly, "Mr. McAuliffe, I've dealt with men like you many times back in the States. When you say you have *our* best interests at heart, I know full well that you really mean that you have the record company's best interest at heart – your bottom line." When McAuliffe opened his mouth to speak, Janet raised her hand to stop him. "There's no need for you to say anything more. You see, *I do* have our best interest at heart. So, because of that, I'll go along with your little charade…stay in the shadows…keep out of the way."

Ian finally spoke. "It's only temporary luv, I promise. We'll be a family soon enough."

Janet said nothing. She felt trapped. Her life had taken a sudden change of direction and she wasn't sure she had the courage to face it.

♫ ♫ ♫ ♫ ♫

Janet gave birth to her daughter in September of 1965. She named the child Danielle in memory of her deceased brother Danny. Her birth certificate read Danielle Cavelli, giving the child her maiden name.

Chapter Six:
"A Chocolate Peanut Roll"

"You were shagging her with a bloody candy bar!" Janet screamed at Ian as she flung the afternoon edition of the *London Daily Word* in his face. He managed to deflect the pages of the oversized tabloid so that they floated to the floor in utter disarray. The front page landed at his feet. He saw the headline printed in bold black typeface.

Have Knot Markham Enjoys a Tasty Treat From Between the Legs of Sexy Starlet!

"That's a damn bloody lie!" Ian defended himself. He picked up the pages and hurled them into the air a second time. "The bleedin coppers made all that up when they couldn't find what they were lookin for."

The story that accompanied the headlines gave many details.

> Last night, London Police raided the Pembroke Manor home of rock star Ian Markham. Acting on an anonymous tip that individuals were selling narcotics, police found nearly a dozen men and women engaged in lewd and lascivious conduct. Markham, lead singer of the rock band the Have Knots, was engaged in oral sex with a blonde female reported to be actress Shelly Francis. The woman had the remnants of a Baum's Chocolate Peanut Roll protruding from her privates. Police confiscated marijuana, prescription drugs, sex toys and other paraphernalia. Summonses were issued but no arrests were made.

Janet continued shouting. "Are you saying Shelly

wasn't here? That she wasn't naked and you weren't…?"

Ian stammered like a child confessing to his parents. "Shelly *was* here. And yes, she got stoned. And when she gets stoned she usually ends up naked…" Shelly Francis was a buxom blonde ingénue featured in several of Hammer Film Productions gothic horror movie remakes. She loved the band and had been at many parties at the estate. "Look, luv, I was a bit out of it myself so the whole scenario is something of a blur. The bulls stormed in, had a look around and got their jollies at seein Shelly in the buff, then went on their merry way. What's the biggie?" Ian actually giggled with his response.

His cavalier comment set Janet off again. "For heaven's sake Ian, our daughter was upstairs in her room!"

Ian went on the defensive. "The tyke slept through the whole affair. Felicia was with her. She'll tell you herself." Felicia Hanratty was Danielle's live-in nanny. She came to the family with impeccable references and worked for them since Danielle was a toddler.

As a result of a stream of hit records and sold out concerts, the Have Knots were near the top of the British musical hierarchy by the end of 1968. It became impossible for Ian to spend time with Janet and their daughter in public.

Dani, as her parents came to call her, had golden blonde hair and sparkling blue eyes that seemed to take in every detail of the circus-like atmosphere that surrounded her. Flashbulbs went off around them wherever they went. Reporters shouted questions about the identity of the woman and child often seen in his company. Ian simply said that Janet was a close friend. He never openly admitted to being Danielle's father. This proved too hurtful for Janet to endure.

Meanwhile, Janet was achieving some notoriety of her own. Her photography books became very popular. Since *The Priory* there had been a second book, *Castles of the Scottish Moors*, published the following year. Germany was explored next in *Ruins on the Rhine*. Her fourth book, *Windmills of the Lowlands*, was due out for the coming holiday season. She accepted assignments to do photo spreads for many major magazines and her work was featured in prestigious art galleries. She was sometimes kept away on assignments, book tours or signings throughout the country which was why she hadn't been home for the debacle of the previous evening.

Ian often took advantage of her absence to schedule his little parties.

It was now apparent that the large mansion in Pembroke Manor could no longer be considered the safe haven they perceived it to be when they leased the place. The ten acre estate set back in the wooded English countryside boasted nearly twenty rooms in all. A huge sunken living room was lavishly furnished and played host to events as diverse as movie nights, jam sessions, séances and contract negotiations. A massive grand staircase situated in a large entryway separated the north and south wing on the second floor.

Janet and Ian shared a master bedroom suite, but she sometimes stayed with Danielle in her large bedroom in the north wing, as would her nanny if the situation warranted. Otherwise, Felicia occupied an apartment of her own on the third floor of the south wing. A handpicked staff consisting of a cook, two housemaids and chauffer all had rooms there as well. The north wing was Ian's domain. He had an office, library and recording studio. Two burly security men and a personal trainer also had third floor bedrooms.

After she calmed a bit she told Ian, "I've made up my mind. I'm moving to an apartment in town and I'm taking Danielle with me."

"Now, now luv. You're overreacting. I told you the tot was sound asleep. She didn't see or hear any of it."

"*This time*. I've warned you about carousing with your drugged up friends and whores while Dani was in the house."

Ian still didn't take her seriously. "Don't get your knickers in a ruffle. Everyone is all amped up about going to the States. This is it luv, the big push. Everything we've planned for. The Ed Sullivan Show. All of it."

At long last, the record company came up with a way to allow the Have Knots to tour in America. Alcohol, drug abuse, and frequent run-ins with the law had dubbed the band as "the bad boys of rock and roll." Some of them missed shows, bringing about cancellations. Cancellations translated into law suits. The company had enough of their behavior and wouldn't finance the tour without first acquiring an insurance bond from an outside company. Having done that, the tour was now just weeks away.

Janet went back on her threat to move out. Ian was right. She too looked forward to the trip to the States. Home.

Chapter Seven:
"John and Tricky Dick"

Despite his campaign promise that he had a secret plan to end the war in Vietnam, President Richard Nixon refused to outline any type of schedule for the withdrawal of troops from Southeast Asia. In May of 1970, he announced that he was escalating hostilities by sending US troops into the tiny nation of Cambodia. Their mission would be to search out and destroy strongholds of troops and material the North Vietnamese kept stored just over the border.

The next day protestors took to the streets in many cities and on college campuses. At Kent State University in Ohio, students set fire to the school's ROTC building, burning it to the ground. State officials called out the National Guard.

Students chanting, "Pigs off campus!" were met by Guardsmen extolling through bullhorns, "For your own safety, all you bystanders and innocent people, please clear the area." The angry crowd of about 500 continued to move forward throwing rocks and cursing at the detachment of 77 soldiers armed with M1 Garand rifles. Inexplicably, a barrage of 67 shots rang out. Four students were killed and a number of others wounded. The entire confrontation lasted a mere thirteen seconds, but the ramifications reverberated worldwide. A gripping photograph of a young woman kneeling over the body of a slain student appeared in newspapers and on magazine covers everywhere. Her mouth was agape in horror and her arms outstretched as if to plead *"Why?"*

♫♫♫♫♫

Upon seeing the photos in *Life* magazine, singer/songwriter Neil Young wrote a song about the incident and called it "Ohio." He hurried into a Los Angeles recording studio with the other members of his group, David Crosby,

Stephen Stills and Graham Nash, to lay down the track for rush-release.

His lyrical depiction of the National Guard as tin soldiers and the direct use of President Nixon's name in association with the line "...four dead in Ohio," led to the banning of the song on many AM radio stations. However, it clearly reflected the ever-evolving consciousness of rock music.

Soon Congress and many state legislatures came under pressure to ratify the 26th Amendment to the Constitution lowering the voting age from 21 to 18. "Old enough to fight...old enough to vote" became a rallying cry. The amendment was signed on July 5, 1971.

A new crop of young Americans were now able to vote.

♫ ♫ ♫ ♫ ♫

Rumors circulated for months throughout the music world that the Beatles were close to disbanding. John Lennon and Paul McCartney continued to share songwriting credits through the release of their LP "Let it Be" in May of 1970. Lennon's compositions were easily discernible by their anti-establishment, anti-war tone. In addition, George Harrison emerged as a prolific composer in his own right and lobbied to have more of his tunes included on their albums. Creative differences between the three abounded. "Let It Be" became the last LP the Beatles would release as a band. The most influential music group in the history of rock and roll dissolved after just a seven year run. All four members planned to pursue solo careers.

With his long hair framing his face, John Lennon appeared Christ-like except for the round steel-rimmed glasses that added a touch of Gandhi to his persona. His composition "Give Peace a Chance" became an anthem for the half-million protestors at the Vietnam Moratorium Day protest in Washington DC in 1969. After moving to New York with his wife, Japanese performance artist Yoko Ono, the couple realized their union was capable of creating great media attention.

Jerry Rubin and Abbie Hoffman, two radical militant activists, saw the potential in having someone like a former Beatle as a spokesman for their cause and attached themselves to the Lennons. At their urging, John performed at rallies and concerts aimed at protesting the government and the war. Mike Douglas, the popular host of a nationally televised afternoon talk show, invited the Lennons to co-host for a week. They picked as their panel of guests, Hoffman and Rubin, Angela Davis and Bobby Seale, the founder of the militant Black Panther Party.

Some people in Washington became very nervous. Senator Strom Thurmond from South Carolina was the chairman of the Senate Internal Security Subcommittee. He sent a secret memo to John Mitchell, the US Attorney General. The memo used information gained by illegal FBI wire taps on the peace movement and their intention to organize a "Political Woodstock."

"…they have devised a plan to hold rock concerts in various primary election sites…" The memo went on to say, "…they intend to use Lennon as a drawing card…" Then concluded, "if his visa is terminated it would be a strategic countermeasure."

A letter was slipped under the door of Lennon's apartment from the Immigration and Naturalization Service. It read:

> Your temporary stay in the United States as a visitor has expired on February 29th 1972. It is expected you will effect your departure from the United States on or before March 15th 1972. Failure to do so will result in the institution of

deportation proceedings.

The reason cited for this action stemmed from John's 1968 arrest and conviction for the possession of cannabis in England.

John appeared nervous when he arrived at the Manhattan office of the INS with his counsel Leon Wildes, an immigration attorney. Lennon feared his telephones were tapped and that he was being followed. Wildes obtained a temporary court order extending John's stay in the US. The Nixon Administration turned up the heat. Lennon told a friend, "All I ever wanted to do was play in a rock and roll band. I can't let them take that away from me."

John and Yoko made public and televised statements that they never intended to travel to either of the convention cities or perform in any kind of protest concert. It became apparent that the peaceniks underestimated the kind of dirty tricks the government would employ to achieve their goals.

♫ ♫ ♫ ♫ ♫

Frank Willis worked as a security guard at the Watergate Business Complex in Washington DC. As he made his rounds on the evening of June 17th 1972, he discovered the latch on a door normally kept locked was taped open. He called the police. They arrested five men for breaking into the office of the Democratic National Committee Headquarters for the purposes of bugging the office and phone lines.

A reporter, Bob Woodward, in his first year at the *Washington Post*, was assigned to cover the arraignment of the five suspects. There, one of the burglars named James McCord, gave his profession as a retired security consultant. When pressed by the judge as to who his former employer was, he replied, "the Central Intelligence Agency." Publishers at the newspaper realized the huge impact of the story. They assigned Carl Bernstein, a reporter with better political contacts within the Beltway, to work with Woodward.

Together they discovered that police had found papers in the burglars' hotel rooms linking them to Howard Hunt, a White House employee on the President's Special Investigation Unit. Further inquiries tied Hunt to Charles Colson, Special Counsel to President Nixon. The reporters also learned of a secret slush fund that dispensed cash from the Committee to Re-elect the President to the burglars. The White House shredded thousands of documents in an effort to cover-up this fact.

Despite the intensity of the investigation, President Nixon was re-elected in a landslide victory in November 1972. But soon after, not even the ongoing Paris Peace Accords aimed at ending the war in Vietnam could turn the tide of public opinion festering against the president.

The US Senate began televised hearings into the Watergate scandal. Witnesses testified to the existence of secret tapes recorded in the Oval Office. To keep the tapes from going public Nixon cited the issue of national security. When forced to produce them, the tapes contained obvious gaps. Many concluded *someone* had tampered with them.

Indictments came down for forty administration officials. Congressional leaders told the president he faced certain impeachment. On August 9, 1974, Richard Nixon resigned from office. Vice-President Gerald Ford was sworn in as the 38th President of the United States.

♫ ♫ ♫ ♫ ♫

By the end of April 1975, it became apparent that the South Vietnamese capital city of Saigon was about to fall making a massive evacuation of American civilians and military personnel necessary. The signal to begin the evacuation was to be the broadcast of Bing Crosby's version of "White Christmas." Someone at Armed Forces Radio forgot to play it. With North Vietnamese troops closing in, thousands of refugees stormed the locked gates of the US Embassy in full panic. Marines virtually lifted women, children, members of the press and foreign nationals over the walls to safety.

As Johnny and Barbara Seracino watched these events play out on the TV in their basement, they were horrified.

"Christ Johnny," Barbara said softly. She didn't expect an answer and didn't get one. "All those poor boys killed or maimed, for this?"

Her husband reflected on the war and the impact it had on the Du-Kanes. Hector Torres was caught evading the draft and sent to Vietnam only to be killed in the Tet Offensive. Kenny Liebermann lost his foot in battle. His best friend Bobby Vitale served in the Navy then started a new life and stayed away from his friends and his hometown for many years. Johnny himself evaded military service only because he had a wife and two children. But Barbara was right; there were tens of thousands of others.

The televised newscast switched its coverage to a camera aboard a US aircraft carrier in the South China Sea. Deck crews unloaded arriving helicopters which had been shuttling refugees and personnel rescued from the Embassy roof. There was more to the story as a newsman on the scene reported. "Somehow, South Vietnamese government officials and their families fearing reprisals have commandeered US military helicopters and flown them to the carriers. Crews are letting people remain on board certainly. But to keep pilots from going back for more unauthorized personnel, the aircraft are being pushed overboard into the sea."

"Tsk, tsk, tsk," Barbara whispered.

This time Johnny did reply, "That's a fucking disgrace."

Chapter Eight:
"Nostalgia"

In 1688, Swiss mercenaries fighting in France and Italy fell victim to a strange malady that reached epidemic proportions. The symptoms included an intense feeling of melancholy, overall weakness in the limbs, loss of appetite and lightheadedness. Doctors likened the disease to homesickness and the strong desire to return to happier times. It was a Swiss medical student who gave the condition its name, "Nostalgia."

Through the centuries, the word evolved to take on a more pleasant and uplifting connotation. People came to embrace and enjoy those things that made them think of the past. Music can be a trigger for a severe sense of nostalgia and by the early 1970's a nostalgia craze was in full swing.

♫ ♫ ♫ ♫ ♫

In Chicago, Jim Jacobs and Warren Casey wrote a play depicting the trials and tribulations of teenage life in high school circa 1959. They called it *Grease*. Producers Ken Waissman and Maxine Fox saw the show and suggested that if the writers added some musical numbers they would take the production to the New York stage.

Grease: The Musical opened on Broadway in 1972 and became an instant smash hit garnering seven Tony Award nominations.

As a highly respected USC graduate film student, George Lucas worked as a camera operator on the Rolling Stones concert film *Gimme Shelter*. He then wrote a screenplay he called *A Quiet Night in Modesto*. The script was based on his experiences as a teenager cruising the streets with his hot rod buddies in 1962.

He pitched the idea to every major studio in Hollywood with no luck, until Universal Studios gave the film a green light and a shoestring budget. With Lucas as director, and a mostly unknown cast, they used synchronized versions of songs from the late fifties and early sixties in lieu of an original music score. After a title change to *American Graffiti*, the film was released in 1973. The movie became a huge critical and box-office success garnering an Academy Award nomination for Best Picture.

The movie also brought a disc jockey named Wolfman Jack to national prominence. The Wolfman, as he became known, was really Robert Smith, a gravelly voiced radio veteran born in Brooklyn, New York. He already gained fame on the West Coast working for the "border blaster" radio station XERX out of Cuidad Acuna in Mexico. He had a pivotal cameo in the film.

Elsewhere on the airwaves, a significant demand continued for stations that played music exclusively from the fifties and early sixties. This demand brought about the creation of the "oldies radio" format.

Radio station KOOL-FM in Phoenix, Arizona became one of the first stations in the country to devote prime-time weekend hours to the oldies market. They hired a record collector named Jerry Osborne. He did his show under the pseudonym Don Coffey. *The Don Coffey Show* aired Saturday and Sunday nights between 6pm and midnight. The playlist was derived from his personal record collection. Before long, his show became so popular that the station hired a woman to take the huge volume of phone requests from listeners. The singing cowboy, Gene Autry, who owned KOOL-FM, gave Osborne free rein to play anything he chose. By the year's end the station switched to an all-oldies format.

A similar situation occurred in Los Angeles, California with KRTH, a local Top-40 station. KRTH's signal could be heard as far south as Tijuana, Mexico, as far west as Santa Barbara and north to Baker, California. The station switched to an oldies format in 1972. They adopted a new handle, K-EARTH. It was named for Earth Day, a celebration of our planet's natural environment. K-EARTH became one of the most listened to radio stations in the country owing in part to the contributions of its highly popular on-air personalities like Brian Bierne.

But perhaps the most significant addition to the oldies radio market occurred in New York City. Radio station WCBS-FM was floundering between an easy listening "young sound" and album rock format. Broadcasting on a frequency of 101.1 MHz transmitted from atop the Empire State Building, the signal was strong enough to reach the entire New York Metropolitan area. Yet, the station failed to capture enough of the area's prime radio market.

At 6am on July 7, 1972, Johnny Michaels, a disc jockey at WCBS, played the song "Runaround Sue" first recorded by Dion in 1961. This heralded the beginning of New York's first 24-hour oldies station. After adopting the oldies format, the station decided to retain most of their on-air personalities. In addition to Michaels, this included morning man Bill Brown, Gus Gossert and Don K. Reed, a deejay who began at the station doing fill-in work for regular jocks out sick or on vacation. In 1973, the station hired Cleveland radio personality Norm N. Nite, also known as Mr. Music, to host a show of doo-wop tunes every Sunday night from 9pm to midnight. It was called *The Nite Train Show*. Nite remained in that spot until he left the station in 1975. The timeslot was then given to Don K. Reed and renamed *The DooWop Shop*.

By turning up the reverb in the studio, Reed's commanding voice sounded like Moses on high. He played all his records on a turntable with the scratches and hisses coming through. This added an aura and sense of nostalgia to the music and harmonies he presented. Listeners phoned in requests. During his last hour he often featured live groups in the studio. His show became a staple in New York radio. Joseph and Janet rarely missed it.

WCBS's main competition in New York was WNBA. They offered Top-40 content on both the AM and FM bandwidths. In 1972, Rich Rosen was promoted to station manager. He dropped the Top-40 format for both stations. They went all-oldies all the time with Jacob Miliewski, in his radio persona of J. Munrow, anchoring two, four hour shows every Friday and Saturday night. Rosen remained on the air on the AM side with his immensely popular *Street Harmony Review*.

As for the rest of the rock and roll audience, the music fragmented into several subgenres. All of them competing for the limited number of slots on the record charts.

Psychedelic rock carried over from the 60s, but began to wane when three top stars, Jimi Hendrix, Janis Joplin and Jim Morrison of the Doors, all died within a year from drug or alcohol abuse. Members of the Grateful Dead and the Have Knots regularly appeared before magistrates and judges answering to charges of narcotics possession and use.

Heavy Metal was a term taken from the lyrics of a song "Born to Be Wild," by Steppenwolf. It was soon used to describe a whole new music genre featuring loud heavily amplified instruments. Some called it "the blues on steroids," which propelled three British bands, Led Zeppelin, Black Sabbath and Deep Purple, to stardom.

Soft rock and folk rock offered a toned down variety of tunes that remained faithful to love songs performed by songwriters and performers like James Taylor, Carole King and Jackson Browne.

After its move to Los Angeles, Motown spearheaded the flourishing soul music market, along a new style simply called funkadelic.

Chapter Nine:
"Happy Days"

At the age of ten, Danielle Rabinowitz loved the American rock band KISS. Its members wore face paint and outrageous costumes. Their stage shows featured pyrotechnics, fire breathing and blood spitting. One of their first big hits was a song called "Rock and Roll All Nite." Being the avid fan that she was, Danielle could explain what every detail of each character meant.

"Paul, he's the Starchild so he has a star painted around one eye and red lipstick. Gene is the Demon so he has devil's wings around his eyes. Ace Frehley is the Spaceman and he has this cool spaced out design on his face. He's my favorite. Peter is the Catman with cat's whiskers and a cat nose."

Like any good mother, Janet paid close attention to the things her daughter enjoyed. On the other hand, Joseph had no real interest in a mid-seventies band that depended more on theatrics than musical ability. Still, he *did* learn a few things from his daughter.

♫♫♫♫♫

On a Tuesday night, just after dinner, Joseph told Janet about a new idea the company was pursuing. They planned to release a series of compilation albums and cassette tapes featuring various artists from the fifties and sixties. The series would be called *Golden Greats*.

"I think that's a terrific idea," Janet said.

"Does that mean you'll be making records again Daddy?" Danielle asked.

"No sweetheart, it just means we'll take old songs by different groups and put them on records and tapes."

Danielle put the thumbs of both hands up in the air and issued a grunt-like groan, "Aaayyh."

Janet got a kick out of the confused look on her

husband's face.

"What's all that?" he asked.

"Daddy don't you know the Fonz?"

"Yeah Dad, everybody knows *the Fonz*," Janet teased.

"What in the world is a Fonz?" He was truly baffled.

Janet tried to explain, "The Fonz, Arthur Fonzarelli, or some such. He's a character on a TV show, *Happy Days*. It's all about the fifties. I think you'd like it."

"It's on tonight," Danielle said excitedly. "Will you watch it with us Daddy?"

"Of course I will sweetheart. I can't go on being the only father in America who doesn't know who the Fonz is, now can I?"

The three of them settled in front of their television set at eight that evening tuned in to the ABC network. From the opening strains of Bill Haley and his Comets singing "Rock Around the Clock," Joseph was hooked. He shared a glance and a smile with Janet certain she too had a flashback memory of their younger days in Cleveland. The song on the TV segued into the *Happy Days* theme song with a similarly bouncy oldies flavor.

Happy Days centered on a fictitious group of teens and adults residing in a suburb of Milwaukee, Wisconsin. The lead characters included Richie Cunningham and his family. Richie was a straight-laced teen with all the coming-of-age problems he could handle. His mentor, Arthur Fonzarelli, or simply the Fonz, was a motorcycle-riding rebel with a black leather jacket and slicked back hair.

Most of the action played out at the local teen hangout, Arnold's Drive-In Malt Shop, where songs by Fats Domino, Connie Francis and Bobby Rydell, among others, played softly from a jukebox in the background. Joseph experienced a more melancholy memory when he took note of one of the cars cruising the drive-in. It was a candy apple red 1940 Ford convertible. It reminded him that his friend Danny wanted to paint his convertible the same color.

Chapter Ten:
"...A Good Man Feelin Down"

Born McKinley Williams, he was one of six children in a family of Negro sharecroppers living outside the Mississippi Delta city of Greenville. As near as anybody could remember, the year was 1887, but it *was* during the torrid heat of summer, his mother definitely remembered that. The family worked a parcel of land belonging to a white man named Cready. They earned a dollar a day for laboring from sunrise to sunset.

By the time he was three years old, McKinley walked high on his tiptoes bouncing along the ground with quick steps. His head darted from side to side with an inquisitive gaze.

"That boy of yours struts around the yard like a cockerel rooster," Jim Cready told the child's father. "I think from here on out I'll call him Chanticleer."

The name stuck and soon everyone called him either that or the shortened more palatable Chanty. He was brought up a Baptist worshipping in a tattered old shack that served as a church not far from the farm.

In their non-working hours, the Williams enjoyed playing music. Chanty with his Jew's harp and his dad on fiddle, while his grandfather played guitar. In between songs, his grandmother regaled them all with stories she handed down about the slave days on the plantation.

At nineteen, Chanticleer accompanied his father and Mr. Cready to the railway station in Greenville to ship an order of cotton. There, he saw a man sitting outside the station playing guitar. Instead of a pick, the man used a small pocketknife on the strings making them wail and screech in a way he never heard before. The sound fascinated him.

"Hey there mister," Chanty called out, "what you call that kinda music you're playin?"

"This here is the blues."

"What's that mean?"

"Sonny, the blues ain't nothin but a good man feelin down."

From that day on Chanty began a love affair with the guitar. His granddaddy taught him the essentials until he became quite adept on the instrument. When his grandfather died at the age of 93, his grandma gave his guitar to Chanty.

Chanticleer married a local girl when he was twenty-two. They had one child, a boy. They were happy and set in their ways until tragedy and devastation struck in 1927.

In April, after weeks of heavy rainfall, the Mississippi River flooded over its banks in a rampage of water equal in force and volume to Niagara Falls. The river swelled to a breadth of over 70 miles, threatening much of the most fertile farmland in the country. Along with thousands of other black families, the Williams were transported to "concentration camps" where men and women alike filled sandbags to reinforce the levees. It was no use. Millions of gallons of water poured through destroying the camps and killing hundreds. Chanticleer was the only member of his entire family to survive.

His life shattered, he traveled north and found work as a farmhand for a cotton combine in Hardin, Kentucky. There he married a widow he met at a church social. She had two children, a boy and a girl. Chanty played guitar for pleasure at home, for worship in church and for extra tip money at a juke joint at the nearby crossroads. His wife did not approve. She believed this sinful activity would put him on a path to damnation.

One spring, a stranger came to Hardin County. He was a tall bespectacled white man who asked a lot of questions about musicians and singers. People were naturally suspicious at first, but after they determined that he wasn't a lawman or revenuer, they listened to what he had to say. His name was John Lomax. He paid a visit to the office of the cotton combine and spoke to a group of the workers, Chanticleer among them.

"I've been commissioned by the Library of Congress in Washington to come down here to record folk songs and spirituals and other material to archive them for posterity. I'd be truly grateful to any of you who would come forward to assist us."

"How would I go about makin these *recordings*?" Chanticleer asked with interest.

"I have the necessary equipment in the trunk of my car," Lomax explained, "I've been setting up at eight o'clock every night in a clearing out back behind the church."

The offer was too tempting to pass up.

♫ ♫ ♫ ♫ ♫

Later that night Chanty went to the clearing where he found a large group of people gathered. He sat quietly in the background while several others took their turn at the process of recording songs for the white man from Washington.

A large horn-shaped object extended beyond the body of Lomax's Plymouth automobile. He told Chanty to stand in front of the horn, identify the song he was going to do and then sing into it. After he finished singing two spirituals from church, Lomax made some adjustments to the equipment and held a 12-inch aluminum disc with great care. He placed a tone arm with a sapphire needle on the edge of the disc. As if by some kind of black magic, the recorded sound now played through the horn. It was scratchy and tinny, but Chanty clearly recognized his own voice. Lomax wanted more.

"You do know *other* songs, more *secular* ones?" he asked.

Chanticleer joked with a hearty laugh. "I knows a bunch more, but I don't see what use any library would have for them."

"Suppose you let me be the judge of that," Lomax

replied.

With a greater sense of confidence Chanticleer performed more songs like "Rock Island Line" and "Annabelle Lee." Then he moved on to some twelve-bar blues tunes of varied tempos about broken-hearted men and mean-spirited women. This was just the type of thing Lomax craved. He brought Chanty back to the clearing for a second night and then a third. After that third session, Lomax offered some advice.

"You're missing out on a great opportunity."

"How's that boss?"

"There's a lot of money to be made singing the blues on the Chitlin' Circuit up north. St. Louis, Chicago all the way to New York if you're so inclined."

The Chitlin' Circuit was a series of venues spread out in the north and east in places safe for Negro performers to play, sing and do comedy. Chanticleer's eyes widened. He never dreamed of seeing any of those big cities. Now this man Lomax made it all sound so easy.

"I got me a wife and family. I can't go runnin off and leave them all alone."

"It's your family I'm thinking about. What man doesn't want to make a better life for his family? You want to spend the rest of your days sweating to make other men rich? You've got a God given talent – be a shame to waste it."

Three days later, over the protests and tears from his wife, McKinley Williams jumped a freight train bound for St. Louis, Missouri.

♫♫♫♫♫

Life on the circuit was hard. Travel proved tedious. The distance between the juke joints, clubs and bars was often quite long. The money he made from one gig might be enough to get him to the next one. Sometimes he hitched a ride or even walked. There were days when he literally sang for his supper, or performed some menial task or chore to help him along the way. He wrote and sent money home to his family whenever he could. Soon, that became almost impossible to do. After reaching Chicago, things did get better.

There he made the acquaintance of a fellow Blues guitarist named Charles Bannister. Charlie was two years his junior and a veteran of the circuit. They shared their knowledge and worked out intricate patterns of playing to achieve a full, almost orchestral sound. He also had the gift of gab. More than a few times he was able to convince juke joint operators and theater managers to hire them both. "Two for the price of one, boss, ya cain't beat dat wit a stick." He framed his proposal in a wide toothful grin.

Not everything Charlie promoted had a wholesome side to it. He was a drinker, anything from nickel beer to sour mash whisky, or bathtub gin. He imbibed in copious amounts and at any time of the day or night. Bannister also had a voracious sexual appetite and often employed the services of two or three prostitutes, or barroom floosies, at the same time. It was Chanticleer's job to entertain the others until his friend was ready to move on to his next conquest. He often rebelled in this role as co-conspirator. However, before long, he was boozing and Tom cattin right alongside Bannister.

♪♪♪♪♪

"Charlie, I need to borrow twenty dollas." Chanty told his roommate. Bannister shaved with a straight razor over a bowl in their cold water flat.

They arrived in New York eight months earlier and secured a steady gig playing in the orchestra at the Moonlight Room, a popular East Harlem nightclub on 122nd Street.

"What in the world you need twenty dollas fer?" Bannister asked without taking his eyes away from his reflection in a small mirror.

"I was over to the music store on West 47th Street when

I seen her." He spoke like a man who'd fallen in love at first sight. "She were sittin right there propped up all waxed and shiny. A Bacon and Day Senorita, dark rosewood finish, the prettiest thing you ever did see from the tip of the headstock down to her smooth bottom."

"A box!" Charles exclaimed. "You goin all crazy out the head over a guitar?"

"Not just any guitar, Charlie, a Senorita. The fella in the store let me try it out. The action on the neck was like silk under my fingers. The tone came out rich and pure like a church organ, I swear."

"All that for twenty dollas?"

"Well, it actually costs sixty…"

"Sixty! Now I know you're crazy. A box like that is way too fancy for cats like us, Chanty – more for them uptown Jazz pickers. You buy that thing and likely as not it'll get busted over some drunk's head in a bar fight."

Chanty would not be deterred. "I got thirty-five saved up. If you loan me twenty, that makes fifty-five. I think the fella will let me have it for that."

"Alright, alright. I s'pose I can't talk no sense into you. I'll lend you the cash. Be better off spent on some good sippin liquor though or a hot piece of trim if you ask me."

Owning the new guitar inspired Chanticleer. After repaying his debt to Bannister he bought the strongest guitar case he could find to protect the instrument. He rubbed the mahogany finish with oil after every performance and always brought his Senorita home with him.

Chanty worked hard and soon became one of the most sought after sidemen in the City.

Chapter Eleven:
"Max Seiderman"

In 1940, the murder of a noted crime boss in one of New York City's most notorious mob families brought about Gugliemo "Gugie" Viola's ascension from "capo" to the new "Don." His reputation for loyalty and ruthlessness would have made any Roman Emperor proud. He was smart enough to understand that in order to succeed he needed to enlist the services of honest businessmen, experts who would give the organization the appearance of legitimacy. It helped if the businessmen had some secret vice or addiction that the mob could use to keep them in line.

One such candidate was Max Seiderman, a handsome and intelligent Jewish accountant from the lower East Side. He graduated from Hunter College with high honors in finance and accounting. After becoming a Certified Public Accountant, Max settled in with a good firm and made a comfortable living. He was married with no children and might have led a simple uncomplicated life if not for his three vices, popular music, the ponies and an inordinate attraction to dark skinned Puerto Rican women. Separately, the vices were innocent enough, but together, at least in Max's case, they proved disastrous.

His mistress, a voluptuous woman named Luz Colon, was tall and shapely. She had long wiry black hair fashioned in a style that cascaded down around her neck to rest across her ample décolletage. She was a dancer and featured singer in one of the more popular Latin nightclubs in Harlem. Luz also had an expensive addiction to heroin.

Max fancied himself as a better than average thoroughbred handicapper and for a time he supported Luz's habit with money he won at the track. After one particularly long losing streak, he found himself in need of cash. His bookie suggested he borrow money from one of Gugie Viola's boys just until his luck turned around. When that didn't happen, Max was in way over his head. He met with Viola to discuss his debt.

"You know, back in thirty-one when the feds arrested Al Capone in Chicago, they didn't get him for murder, bootlegging or smuggling. He went away for income tax evasion, ten fucking years. I could use a smart man like you in my operation, just to do the thing you do best, keeping books. One set for me and one for the feds."

"I don't know Mr. Viola," Max's voice quaked with fear, "I've never been involved in anything illegal like that."

"You're into me for a lot of money. That Puerto Rican junkie you're banging likes heroin better than she likes her rice and beans. Problem with a broad like that is even if you was to settle your debt, she'd just run it up again by shootin that shit in her arm. Only way I see you gettin clear of this is if you get rid of the bitch."

"But I love her Mr. Viola. I couldn't do anything like that."

"It would be a shame to mark up her pretty face...maybe fuck up her voice by pouring bleach down her throat."

"Mr. Viola...you wouldn't..."

"It's been known to happen," Gugie answered. "Of course, maybe your wife has that kinda money stashed away under your mattress at home. I could send somebody to check?"

"No...no...please, we have to keep my wife out of this."

"I thought you Jews were supposed to be smart. You see Max, I'm like the Pope in matters like these, fucking infallible. I pass my hand across this table and your debt is absolved, vig and all. Luz can stay high as a kite and Mrs. Seiderman is none the wiser."

Both men knew there was really no choice in the matter. With a handshake, Max Seiderman made his pact with the devil.

As time passed, a true bond of loyalty and trust formed between the two men. In the summer of 1942, Max recruited several graduates from top business schools promising draft deferments to keep them off the battlefields in Europe and out of the jungles of the Pacific.

Max devised a system whereby each of the accountants under him handled only a small portion of the Viola family business. That way, no one individual knew too much about any illegal activity. They could cause no real harm if arrested. It was a stroke of genius on Max's part and Gugie Viola rewarded him handsomely.

He gave Max free rein over the family interests in local jazz clubs and drinking establishments within his territory. Luz Colon died of a drug overdose in 1943. Though Max was crushed he soon moved on. He loved rubbing elbows with the celebrities who performed in the clubs.

♪♪♪♪♪

"Roll me some reefer, will you Maxie?" The light-skinned black female singer asked from across the room. She sat at her dressing table rotating toward him with her request. Her performance wig lay on the table in front of her. She had short, closely cropped hair accentuating her sharp facial features. With the right application of stage makeup, she was considered beautiful. She wore a sheer white silk slip. Her nipples stood taut against the fabric. The hem rose high on her thighs catching the eye of the men also in the room.

One of the men, Milton Thornberry, was a wealthy financier dressed in black tie and tails. Max invited him backstage when he learned that this torch singer was a particular favorite of his. Skelly Taylor, the singer's latest squeeze, was also present. Taylor was a local black street player. He wore a pimpish pinstriped suit and smiled like a loon revealing one gold front tooth. On the surface, Max tolerated people like Skelly. Inwardly, he considered him just *another greasy nigger hanger-on.*

"Really Max? You a toker?" Skelly teased.

"Nah, nah, Skelly," the singer injected, "Maxie don't partake but he do roll a mean joint, doncha Max?"

"Whatever you say honey." Max handed a fat marijuana cigarette to the singer. She lit it, took a deep drag and inhaled a good portion of the smoke as she leaned back in her chair. Her eyes were glassy from the brandy and cocaine she had already ingested. She passed the joint to Thornberry who declined it. Skelly Taylor snapped it up in a flash. The singer continued, "Maxie got some powerful friends gonna help put my career back on track."

Max beamed at the compliment. "I'll do my best sweetheart, you know that."

Thornberry then stood, reached inside his trousers pocket and retrieved a fifty-dollar bill. He folded it and walked over to the dressing table. "I hope you'll do me the honor of singing that song during the next set?" He deftly placed the money down the front of her slip. It lodged deep in her cleavage. She smiled at him.

Max answered for her, "You can be assured she will Mr. Thornberry and you're in for a real treat. Nobody sings 'God Bless the Child' like Billie Holiday."

She made good on the promise in her final set of the evening. The houselights dimmed as the singer sauntered up to the microphone. The newly arranged intro for her signature song featured a tortured guitar riff that rang forth from the belly of a great crafted instrument, a Bacon and Day Senorita played to flawless perfection by a master musician, Chanticleer Williams.

Chapter Twelve:
"Kentucky Revisited"

More than twenty years had passed since Joseph was last in Kentucky. He'd been honorably discharged from the Army after recovering from the serious injuries he suffered in the car crash that killed his best friend Danny Cavelli. On his last day in the Bluegrass State, he boarded a bus to Cleveland, Ohio to visit Danny's grave. The events that followed put his life on a new path.

Now, he sat in the back seat of the car he hired to take him around the city of Radcliff and surrounding area. He avoided Fort Knox, the base where he and Danny had been stationed. A quick drive passed the spot on the stretch of highway where the black pick-up truck ran Danny's convertible off the road showed nothing to mark the incident.

There was also little to see at the place where the Texaco filling station once stood. Though the tall white post remained, partially rotted and unpainted for years, the five-sided Texaco star was gone. The service bays and office were shuttered and overgrown with weeds. A burned out ruin of a small house stood further back on the property. It was there that Joseph spent many an afternoon with Chanticleer Williams, the station's owner and guitarist whose mastery of R&B music became such a passion with him.

"I'd like to go to Harrison Road," Joseph told the driver.

"The old Boyette farm? Ain't much more to see there either."

"I realize that."

The driver shrugged his shoulders. "You're the boss."

The driver was right. The original farmhouse, located several hundred yards from the turnoff, had long ago fallen into disrepair and been boarded up. A smaller add-on structure Teddy built for his parents during the height of his career was closed up as well, though much more recently.

Joseph left the car and walked onto the wooden porch of the house. The rock and roll singer Teddy Boyette was well known for his warmth and homespun innocence despite the hard edge his songs sometimes displayed. Standing now in the place where the singer was raised gave Joseph a good feeling.

He looked around and noticed a small fenced in area not far from the house. Sensing he knew what he'd find there, he headed off in that direction. It was the Boyette family graveyard. Inside the fence he found five headstones. Two were small weathered stone markers standing side by side. The names of Seaford and Emma Boyette, Teddy's paternal grandparents were chiseled across the front. Two more recent marble headstones were those of Teddy's parents. His mother, Jean survived her husband George by three years before passing on herself last January.

The largest, more ornate headstone bore Teddy's name, the dates of his birth and death and a line from one of his early hit tunes written by Joseph and Janet, *a vow that is borne of love transcends all measure of time.*

"He's not really buried there." A strong female voice from behind gave him a start. He spun around to find a young girl standing a short distance away. She was a pretty brunette, dressed in cut-off jeans and a checkered sleeveless blouse. Her arms were folded in front of her. She wasn't wearing a bra. "Teddy, I mean. It's just an empty coffin. Back then folks was afraid some kids might mess with the grave, so they moved his body to the cemetery in Radcliff not long after he died." Joseph was aware of that fact. The girl continued, "I'm Renni Granger. My folks own a farm up yonder a ways. I been looking out for Missus Boyette since her husband passed. Jean loved to talk about her boy. Are you here for the auction?"

"Yes I am," Joseph answered.

The foundation overseeing Teddy's estate had hired the young woman to act as a companion for Teddy's mom. Since the singer's death in 1959, the farm had been turned into a museum of sorts displaying many items collected during his most successful years. The museum was funded by the county and became a major tourist attraction. Like so many other small towns, Radcliff currently suffered from serious economic hardships. The museum was about to close. Curators gathered any items of real value like stage costumes, photographs, awards and musical instruments that were to be sold at an auction the next day. Teddy's Bacon and Day guitar was among those items.

Chanty had given the young singer his guitar for luck when Teddy first went to New York. He used it on his early recording sessions, television appearances and tours. Soon after, Teddy's manager Cap Stewart and Leo Klein negotiated a merchandising deal with the Wilson Guitar Company. Wilson unveiled a handsome, Teddy Boyette SJ-6 model guitar which quickly became popular with musicians everywhere. From that time on, Teddy felt compelled to use the signature instrument himself. The Senorita was sent back to Teddy's home. It remained there until it was packed up and sent to town for the auction. Officials expected it to be the most popular item up for bid.

Joseph had come back to Kentucky for the sole purpose of acquiring the guitar. He placed a high sentimental value on the instrument. Now, with no one in the Boyette family left to claim it, Joseph wanted it no matter the cost.

"Mister," the young girl asked, "you think there's any chance the foundation will keep me on to look after things here?"

"I don't know. That's for them to decide." Joseph told her a little white lie. He knew that after the auction, the foundation was giving up all interests in Kentucky. He didn't want to be the one to disappoint her. "I'm sure someone will let you know. It was nice to meet you Renni."

The girl smiled as Joseph turned to go.

"Lyin bastard," she muttered to herself when he was

out of earshot.

♫ ♫ ♫ ♫ ♫

The hired car drove Joseph to the law offices of Kingman and Halston in Radcliff. There he was met by Harold Kingman the senior partner in the local firm. Marlene-Klein Sussman stood at his side. For the past several years, Marlene, the daughter of Leo Klein, handled all legal matters for Chanticleer Enterprises. She proved herself a smart, capable and confident attorney on a par with any male lawyer of her age and experience.

However, now she appeared shaky and nervous as she approached Joseph. "There's a problem," she said.

"What's wrong?"

"The Senorita is missing."

Joseph looked at Kingman. "Missing? How could something like this happen?"

The gray haired attorney stood speechless. Finally, Marlene spoke on his behalf. "Mr. Kingman's people did an exhaustive inventory. They checked and double-checked every item two days ago. I watched them, with my own eyes, put that guitar in its case and then into a crate. It was transported here with the last of the items yesterday. Today when we opened it, this is what we found."

Kingman motioned to a nearby table where an open guitar case sat. He picked up the instrument contained inside the case, a very old Sears and Roebuck acoustic Silvertone guitar with a worn ash finish. "It must have been switched sometime after we crated it. Though, I don't see how."

"Who else was in the house when you did the inventory?" Joseph asked.

"One or two workers, a security guard…that's about it," Kingman answered.

"No one else, you're sure?"

"Oh…yes, I almost forgot. That nice local girl who

worked for Mrs. Boyette, she was there too."

Renni Granger.

Within the hour, sheriff's deputies were at the Granger farm. Joseph doubted they'd find any trace of Renni or the guitar. He was right. Though they discussed the possibility of postponing the auction, they decided to go on as planned. However, Joseph was determined to get to the bottom of this mystery even if it meant remaining in Kentucky for a prolonged period of time.

♫ ♫ ♫ ♫ ♫

The seating capacity for the main meeting room at the Parsons Avenue Elks Club was approximately seventy-five. Every seat was filled. Veteran memorabilia collectors and dealers assembled and were given a catalog listing all items up for bid. Each was issued a green fan-like paddle with a number stenciled on it to identify the bidder. Joseph and Marlene sat in the front row directly in the center of the room. Photographers and members of the press stood along both sidewalls and filled the area flanking the solid oak doors.

The auctioneer, a thin frail looking man with steel-rimmed glasses may have honed his skills at county fairs and livestock events. He possessed a voice several times his size that boomed and projected to the back of the room with ease. He banged a gavel loudly to get the auction under way.

It took two hours to go through the entire catalog. Some items went quickly, pieces of clothing from Teddy's youth, impossible to authenticate, sold for very little. However, photographs, especially if they were autographed, brought on rabid bidding. One black and white eight-by-ten signed picture of Teddy with the movie star Elizabeth Taylor sold for twelve hundred dollars.

A hush of anticipation rose as the crowd awaited a glimpse of the last item, the Bacon and Day guitar. Murmurs and confused glances circulated as a nervous Harold Kingman stepped to the podium switching places with the auctioneer. "Thank you ladies and gentlemen. This concludes today's auction. On behalf of..."

The rustling and chatter grew until a voice called out from near the door.

"Now, hold on there hoss..." everyone turned. They saw a scruffy young man of about twenty standing in the doorway. He held a guitar over his head, Teddy's Senorita. "I think we got one more piece of business to conduct, the crown jewel of the Teddy Boyette collection."

Flashbulbs popped and a loud grumbling filled the hall.

"Arrest that boy!" Kingman shouted. Security guards moved quickly to carry out the order. The boy switched his grip on the instrument to hold it like a baseball bat threatening to smash it against the nearest hard surface.

"Wait!" Joseph's voice rang out. The security men froze. "Let's hear what he has to say." Then he spoke to the boy. "Why don't you come up here so we don't have to shout."

The young man rested the guitar on his shoulder. "All right. Just everybody keep real still and don't do nothin foolish. We wouldn't want anything to happen to this valuable item now would we?"

As he made his way forward, Joseph noticed Renni Granger following behind him. Joseph got a better look at the boy as he drew near.

He was tall, solidly built with long matted dark hair that fell down to his shoulders in the back. A moustache and short beard framed his mouth and chin. As he walked by, he had words for Joseph.

"I know who *you* are. I seen your picture lots of times. You're Joe Rabin. You brung Teddy Boyette up to New York and made him a big star. Maybe cause of that you figure you got the right to own this here guitar?" He taunted Joseph and enjoyed every moment of it. "But tell me something, can you even play a guitar?"

"No I can't. But what makes you think *you* have any right to it?"

"Maybe I got the right because…Teddy Boyette was my daddy."

Chapter Thirteen:
"TJ"

Flashbulbs continued to go off and the noise level rose. Harold Kingman raised his hand to re-establish some semblance of order. When everyone returned to their seats, the young man stood at the podium ready to make a statement.

"My name is Teddy James Russell but I prefer to go by my initials, TJ. I was born in Tulsa, Oklahoma in December, nineteen fifty-seven. My mama's name was Dolores but everybody called her Dee. At one time she was a waitress at the Olympia Coffee Shop in Memphis, Tennessee. That's where she met Teddy Boyette." The boy spoke in a calm even tone of voice that seemed to give credence to the things he said. "To hear my ma tell it, he was a punk ass down on his luck singer, tried to bully his way into seeing record executives on Music Row. She had a soft spot for boys like him. So she staked him to some clothes, took him in and gave him a place to stay. Then he took advantage of her."

Joseph shook his head and leaned forward in his chair. Many details of Teddy's early life were published in books and magazines, already a matter of public record. In those early days, he and Leo Klein handled all of Teddy's publicity. Neither of them ever heard of a waitress named Dee. The person this TJ described seemed nothing like the young man Joseph knew.

"It was my ma that first introduced him to Cap Stewart," TJ continued. "She asked Cap to give him a break and put him on one of his shows. Once Teddy became popular, it was Cap told him to go back on the promises he made to her. He left her high and dry. When Teddy left to go up north, she was heart broke. My ma left Memphis and went to Oklahoma before she even knew she was pregnant with me. After I was born, she married a trucker who gave me his name and raised me as his own."

Joseph knew that Cap Stewart, Teddy's mentor and personal manager, was a shrewd promoter. He was quite capable of keeping things quiet even if it meant hiding details that may have harmed his protégé.

"TJ," one of the reporters called out, "when did you find out Teddy Boyette was your father?"

"Now hang on there just a second," Kingman interrupted, "we're not going to turn this into some kind of press conference. Fact is this here boy stole that guitar. He's a thief. If he's got a notion he's got some right to have it, he shoulda showed up here and bid on it just like everybody else…" A roar of mock laughter met his remark. "We've listened to his story but none of that excuses his behavior today." Kingman looked directly at the boy. "Young man, my advice to you is to surrender that guitar and take your medicine."

TJ nodded before responding, "You let me have my say and that's really all I came here for anyway. So okay, you can have the dang thing."

He handed the guitar to a security guard. Sheriff's deputies moved quickly to take the boy into custody.

Kingman added, "Arrest that young woman too. She's an accomplice."

One of the deputies grabbed Renni.

"There's no need for that," TJ protested, "she didn't have nothin to do with this. I only used her to get what I wanted."

Kingman again tried to quiet the crowd. "We'll hold these proceedings over until tomorrow at noon, at which time we'll auction off the Bacon and Day guitar."

His announcement fell on mostly deaf ears as many of the press were now more interested in the couple being carted off.

Joseph, Marlene and Kingman moved to a small office off to the side of the main room. "I wouldn't be in such a rush to lock those kids up," Joseph told the attorney.

"Mr. Rabinowitz, Teddy Boyette is a legend in these parts. I don't need to tell *you* that. I'm not gonna sit still and listen to a punk like that tarnish his name. I'm gonna haul his ass in front of a judge. But, I guess I got no problem cutting the girl loose."

"He needs to be taught a lesson, I agree," Joseph said, "but as far as the things he said about Teddy… The fact is, there's no way to refute any of it."

"Nor substantiate it," Marlene added. "If they were things his mother told him its hearsay pure and simple. It wouldn't stand up in any court I know of."

"I agree," Kingman added.

"He wanted a forum, we gave him one," Joseph concluded. "We should talk to him and find out exactly what it is he's after." He aimed his attention to Marlene, "I want you to find out everything you can about this kid, the smallest detail, and the mother too."

"Will do," Marlene answered.

♫ ♫ ♫ ♫ ♫

After fending off a flurry of questions from reporters, Joseph managed to break away and walk to the Sheriff's office where Harold Kingman waited.

Kingman told Joseph, "I took your advice and sent that Renni girl home to her family with a stern warning."

Sheriff Todd McMichael, a gray haired man of about fifty, offered more, "She's from good local folk. I'll ride out there later on and have a talk with her pa. He'll probably take a strap to her, which is worse than anything I could do."

His remark made Joseph smile. "What about the boy?"

"He's been real quiet," the sheriff answered. "I got him sittin inside. I'll lock him up if that's still what you have a mind to do?"

"I'd like to have a talk with him before we do that, if

that's okay?" Joseph asked.

The sheriff answered, "Fine by me."

Kingman just nodded.

The sheriff took Joseph back to where TJ sat. His posture with his legs extended beneath a table, screamed arrogance and disdain for authority. A lit cigarette dangled from the fingers of his right hand. The boy sat up straight when Joseph took a seat opposite him.

"I suppose you're pretty riled at me for crashing your little party like that?" the boy said.

"You know how to make an entrance, I'll give you that." Joseph looked deeply into his eyes, searching for the slightest resemblance between him and Teddy Boyette. He didn't see it.

"What's gonna happen to Renni?" TJ asked.

"They let her go. I guess she's sort of special to you?"

The boy shook his head. "A means to an end is all. I needed her to get access to the guitar. She was pretty sure the Foundation was gonna let her go after the auction. She didn't mind goin along with my little prank. But I am glad she got clear of it."

"Mind if I asked you a few questions?"

"Fire away."

"First of all, I'd like to hear the answer to the question that reporter started to ask you earlier, about when you first found out that Teddy was your father?"

The young man took a deep drag on his cigarette and leaned back. "Guess I was about nine. Ben Russell, the trucker who raised me, started taking me out with him on short hauls. Ole Ben always figured I'd end up truckin like him. He had a radio in his rig, and he sang along to all the country tunes..." TJ chuckled at this apparent happy memory, "...I learned the words to them songs better than I learned the roads 'round Tulsa. He told my mama I had a good voice and it wasn't long before I started singing for her as well."

He spoke of how his mother told him he was the son

one of the most famous rock and roll singers there ever was. She had collected every record Teddy Boyette ever made. When her husband was out on the road, she played them for her son. It was the tearful details of her stories about Teddy's abandonment that angered him.

"I decided I'd be the one to make it all up to her. By the time I was fifteen, I learned to play guitar and was singin with other guys, but I never said nothin bout who I was. My mama died in seventy-three. Russell tossed me out on my ear when I told him truck drivin wasn't for me. I been on my own ever since."

"Your story would be a lot easier to believe if you had some kind of proof."

"Well, answer me this, if it wasn't true, why would Cap Stewart pay my mama hush money every month?"

"Cap paid your mother money?"

TJ nodded, "Right up until the time that plane crashed." Teddy Boyette, Cap, and everyone in Teddy's band died in a plane crash while on tour in Florida in 1959.

"You have proof of that, about the money?"

"I have letters."

"I'd like to see those."

"In a week's time, everybody can see them."

The boy's answer confused Joseph, "What happens in a week?"

"That's when Artie Franklin announces that he's signing my band to Myriad Records." TJ smiled and sat back in his chair, confident that this last piece of information struck Joseph like the blow of a hammer.

Joseph knew Teddy had run afoul of Franklin, in his first days in Memphis, and how the executive tossed Teddy out of his office. It seemed Franklin, now in his seventies, wasn't going to make the same mistake twice and miss an opportunity to sign Teddy's son.

♫ ♫ ♫ ♫ ♫

Joseph rejoined Kingman and the sheriff in the outer office.

"Appears you two had lots to talk about," the sheriff noted.

Joseph directed his response to Kingman, "I think we should let him go."

"What?" Kingman showed surprise. "Why?"

"He claims to have some sort of proof, letters from Cap Stewart to his mother. And, as it turns out, this whole thing was just a publicity stunt cooked up by Artie Franklin. He's signing the kid's band to a contract. If we lock him up it only draws more attention to him, which is what he wants. We got the Senorita back. We should just leave it at that."

Kingman shook his head as if in defeat. "I'll go along with anything you say Joseph, but I got a feeling we haven't heard the last from that punk."

Joseph agreed.

He did accomplish one positive thing on his trip to Kentucky. At the auction the next day, he outlasted two staunch competing bidders and came away with the treasured Senorita.

Chapter Fourteen:
"Danielle's Discovery"

"That's the most incredible thing I've ever heard."

Janet's reaction to the story about Teddy's alleged son was about what Joseph expected. He telephoned her the night of the auction and gave her a rather sketchy report on the incident. Now, three days later, seated in the dining room of their home, she wanted to hear every detail her husband could recall.

The information was fleshed out by facts Marlene Klein learned through her investigation. As she told Joseph, "Mr. Kingman's people in Memphis went to the Olympia Coffee Shop. It's still there and still open for business. They even have a plaque behind the counter telling how Teddy Boyette ate there when he first came to town. Anyway, there's a waitress who works there now whose mother, a woman named Paula, worked there years ago and *she* remembers the woman Dee."

"Did they talk to this *Paula*?" Joseph asked.

"No, but they did get a telephone number so *I* called and spoke to her," Marlene paused before relaying good news. "She has quite a different take on the tale this TJ is spinning."

As Marlene relayed it, Dee was a woman who on occasion had no qualms about flirting with handsome younger men. In some cases she even seduced them. "According to Paula, that's what happened with Teddy. She said that Teddy's meeting Cap Stewart that first day was purely coincidental. Dee had nothing to do with it, other than she waited on both men at the counter. She *did* bring him home and bought him clothes and things, but that was solely part of her seduction. When Teddy became popular, Dee became clingy and thought of him as her meal ticket out of Memphis. After Teddy went to audition in New York, Dee left Tennessee. Paula never heard from her again and insisted she never knew Dee was pregnant."

"And this boy claims to have letters?" Janet asked.

Joseph nodded. "One letter, written to his mother from Cap Stewart in which Cap agrees to send cash every month for the boy's upbringing in return for her keeping silent about the entire situation. After that, just some empty envelopes from Cap's address in New York."

"Sounds more like blackmail to me."

"Without any other concrete proof of what she was saying, I guess his mother was satisfied with what she got. It all ended after Teddy and Cap were killed."

"And no one at the record company knew anything?"

"I certainly didn't."

"And Leo?"

"No," he said with great affirmation. Joseph questioned Leo once before on a similar matter. He vowed never to do so again, though he would now discuss this matter with his partner.

Janet sat in thought for a moment. "Joseph, do you think Teddy knew?"

Joseph shook his head. "He wasn't capable of such a thing. If he'd known he would have come forward and taken responsibility."

"Why is some man saying such bad things about Teddy?" Danielle's voice from behind caused them to turn and see their eleven year old standing near the entrance to the dining room. She had no real memory of the singer, yet she *was* aware of his connection to her family through his records and the things she read about.

"We don't know sweetheart, but this man could just be making it all up," Janet told her.

"I bet he is," Danielle answered. "Teddy couldn't do anything so very bad."

"I agree with you Dani," Joseph said.

"And he was really funny too."

"Did you see him being funny on an old TV show?" her mom asked.

"No, he's funny when he talks on the tapes."

"What tapes sweetheart?" Joseph asked.

"The big ones we have in the basement."

Joseph looked at his wife who merely shrugged her shoulders. Danielle had a favorite game she enjoyed when she played alone in the house she called it Disc Jockey. Joseph had a lot of old records and tapes stored in their basement. There was a record player and a reel to reel tape recorder that Joseph set up and taught her how to use.

"Can you show me these tapes sweetheart?"

"Sure."

The three of them went down into the basement. For the most part everything was neatly arranged. Cardboard boxes, many unopened for years, were stacked atop one another. Danielle played in an area where a card table for the portable record player and tape recorder were located.

"Did you find the tapes in one of those?" Joseph asked, pointing to a stack of boxes.

"Um-hum," Danielle answered, "those two over there."

Joseph looked and saw two boxes with the word AMPEX emblazoned on the side.

A vague and distant memory came to his mind. Images arose from years ago on the last day at the Brill Building offices of Chanticleer Records. It was a farewell lunch with Leo, Mickey Christie and Curtis Tinnsley. The memory expanded to something Mickey said, words to the effect of, *I left a couple of boxes with your secretary...tapes from the Bronx days...some stuff we played around with.*

"Is that the tape that's in the machine now?" he asked Danielle.

"Yes...want me to play it?"

"Sure go ahead."

"Okay." Still very much a part of the game to the youngster, she took up position in a metal folding chair and assumed the role of disc jockey. "And now folks, here he is, Teddy Boyette."

Danielle switched on the recorder. The ensuing voices coming through the small built-in speaker took Joseph and Janet back nearly twenty years.

You shake your ass like that when you're on stage? Joseph thought hard…that was the voice of Raymond, the bass player in Curtis' combo.

Course I do. The chicks go crazy for it, man. There was no mistaking that voice. It was Teddy and this was his audition tape.

The sound of a group of boys laughing followed. Danielle smiled when she turned to see her mother move closer to Joseph's side. He put his arm around her shoulder.

Are you kidding? Dean Martin is like a God in my house… This was Freddie Christie's response to Teddy asking if the group knew any Dean Martin songs.

They listened as Teddy sang Dean Martin's rendition of the old standard "You Belong to Me." His touching and heartfelt performance surprised everyone back then. Even now, decades later, it had an effect on these three listeners. Tears rolled down Janet's cheeks. When the song finished Danielle clicked off the tape machine.

"Did I do something wrong Daddy?" she asked with profound innocence.

"No, Dani not at all."

"Then why is Mommy crying?"

Janet dabbed her cheeks dry with the backs of her hands and bent to embrace her child. "It's just that I get very emotional when I remember how it was being there when Teddy did this."

Danielle's eyes widened. "You were there, Mommy, right there with them?"

"Yes, and Daddy was too."

"Wow! That's so cool. There's plenty more to hear."

"I know that sweetie," Joseph said. "Tomorrow when

you get home from school I want to listen to all there is. What you found here could be very valuable. If it is then I think on Saturday, you and I will take a train ride into Manhattan and bring the tapes to a recording studio. I'll have an engineer put it all on cassettes for you. Would you like that?"

Danielle beamed. "Oh yes, cassettes are easier to play and I can bring them to my room."

🎵🎵🎵🎵🎵

Well provisioned with two peanut butter and jelly sandwiches, a plate of Oreo cookies and two tall glasses of milk, Joseph and Danielle were back in the basement the next afternoon. Joseph was treated to a real surprise, a tape recording of Teddy he never heard before. To his recollection he, Leo Klein, and Cap Stewart, had gone upstairs to negotiate Teddy's first contract. The boys remained in the basement performing a jam session. Mickey Christie had the good sense to record it all, an hour's worth of material, banter and conversation no fan had ever heard and no radio station ever played.

Father and daughter listened to a second tape and then a third before Janet called them for dinner. Afterward, she joined them to listen along to hour after hour of raw material. Sometimes Teddy played alone with his guitar, while learning the words and arrangements to new songs Joseph and Janet wrote for him. There were alternate takes on songs that would top the national record charts in a completely different form. The tapes contained outtakes, mistakes and banter between the artist and the members of his band. On occasion, Joseph's voice came through encouraging and sometimes even chiding Teddy to sing with more feeling or change the way he phrased certain lyrics.

By the time the fourth tape finished, Danielle was asleep, curled up on a throw pillow and covered with a blanket.

"How many more are there?" Janet asked.

"Six. But I don't need to hear any more. If they're anything like the others we've struck the mother lode. There's enough for a boxed set, unreleased material and alternate takes. Collectors will go crazy for it."

"So, what's the next step?"

"I'll call Leo tomorrow and bring him up-to-date."

Janet sensed more. "You've got something on your mind. I can tell."

"Nothing I want to share just yet, not until I talk to an expert."

♫ ♫ ♫ ♫ ♫

The expert turned out to be his sound engineer Mickey Christie in California. After exchanging pleasantries via the telephone Joseph told Mickey about the tapes.

"Yeah, yeah, I remember them boxes. In your basement all these years you say? Wow, I'm surprised they didn't oxidize," Mickey commented with a laugh.

Joseph went on to tell his friend about what he had in mind.

Mickey proved most helpful and encouraging. "It's been done before. I remember hearing how they filled out some tracks Buddy Holly recorded before he died and released them as singles afterward." Holly partially recorded three songs, "True Love Ways," "It Doesn't Matter Anymore" and "Raining in My Heart" four months prior to his death. They were released posthumously with added musical tracks. Mickey continued, "Back when we worked in the Bronx, that old Presto machine only had four tracks. These days we're using sixteen. It could get real interesting. Who are you going to get to do it?"

"Well, I was hoping…"

The sound of Mickey's laughter on the line told Joseph he got the hint. "Okay, Linda has been after me to go back east and visit her folks. I tell you what, you put us up in that fancy mansion you got there in Westchester and we can be there in a week."

It was Joseph's turn to laugh. "You got a deal."

🎵🎵🎵🎵🎵

An extended visit with old friends excited Janet. She was also thrilled to learn about Joseph's plan to make a new release using Teddy's voice.

"It is rather timely don't you think?" she asked him.

"How so?"

"I mean with this kid TJ about to break on the scene and bring all this negative publicity about Teddy. Don't you feel in some way that by putting together this box set, you're counteracting all that, reinforcing the positive things about him?"

"I didn't really think about it in that way."

Janet made a face and let out a breath. Her visage displayed that she knew her husband better than that.

"Okay," he admitted, "maybe I do enjoy the idea of stealing this kid's thunder and putting things right. Am I wrong?"

Janet shook her head. "Teddy needs a champion. Who better than you?"

Chapter Fifteen:
"Genius At Work Revisited"

After sending the wives and kids out for a Westchester County shopping spree, Joseph and Mickey listened to the raw material on the Ampex tapes.

"So is this the ultimate example of déjà-vu or what?" Mickey quipped.

"You mean being in the basement?" Joseph got it.

"Seems like you and I do some of our best work in places like this."

Both men laughed.

The veteran sound engineer was equally impressed by what he heard. They made copious notes and discussed what material they could best make use of. There were complete tunes recorded start to finish that for some reason never got released. If it was because of a technical problem, Mickey felt sure he now had the wherewithal to fix it in the editing process. These songs would hold a special interest to Teddy's fans.

They discovered true gems; alternate takes of familiar songs done in a different tempo or with different backing vocals or harmonies. The same for outtakes, those spontaneous moments in a session when someone made a mistake that caused parts of an in-studio conversation to come through and were always fun. *Wooded Chapel, take fifteen*, was one of Joseph's favorites. Mickey had his own.

Okay, guys let's settle down in there. Mickey's voice spoke to Teddy and Curtis' combo in an early session. Once all was quiet, a piano and tenor saxophone started to play some notes.

Okay, Teddy is heard to say as he clears his throat.

Quiet, boys! Mickey shouted, more admonishing this time. Once he had the silence he needed, he spoke again, *pitch, Freddie.* This was Mickey's cue to his brother Freddie, the piano player, to give Teddy his starting note, a C.

♪ ♪ ♪ ♪ ♪

Joseph booked an ample amount of studio time at the Wax Trax Record Plant, a state-of-the-art recording facility in mid-town Manhattan. As a further reward for discovering the lost material, Joseph brought Danielle along for the first three daytime sessions. She sat quietly in the large control booth totally mesmerized by the work.

A four-piece horn section and a string ensemble were brought in. Joseph wanted all instruments, no synthesizers or drum machines to intrude on the purity of the original material. Curtis Tinnsley arrived from the coast to direct the musical portion of the operation. Quite fitting since he too had been present on those early recordings. The uncanny bond between these three creative minds was most evident. They worked as one to bring forth new musical arrangements, which melded with the original vocal tracks to create seamless recordings as though they were made at the exact same time, not more than twenty years later.

Joseph had come to appreciate the work Elvis Presley did in Nashville, Tennessee with a background group called the Jordanaires. When Teddy recorded his hit "Within a Wooded Chapel," the Pixies, featuring Evie Rhodes, did the backup vocals. For the box-set version, Joseph wanted to replace the female vocal tracks and use the Jordanaires. He brought the group to New York for a two-day session where Mickey overdubbed their background vocals with great success.

As the work became more intricate, Joseph and Mickey worked alone sometimes long into the night re-mixing the tracks. Some of the older recordings had flaws, hissing, popping and other audible noise which was why they were left out in the first place. Working now with sixteen tracks and painstaking precision, Mickey was able to remove a good amount of noise to achieve just the right balance of sound.

The expert engineer plied the tools of his trade like a

surgeon. Using the newest editing console with a calibrated motor and a system called Sel-Sync, he had the ability to change keys by slowing down the tape. He could also listen to a specific word or inflection on the play head, insert an edit using the record head and synchronize it perfectly.

For the more standard edits Mickey lined up the tape at the precise numeric position where he wanted to make the cut and marked it with a pen. He then removed the tape from the recording head and put it in a wooden splicing block to hold it securely. Mickey used a sharp knife with an angled blade to slice the thin tape evenly. He then placed a small piece of splicing tape over the two edges and squeezed the edit firmly. The process was repeated over and over until the entire project was done.

♫♫♫♫♫

The day Mickey and his family flew back to California, trade periodicals across the country ran the story that Myriad Records out of Memphis had signed a new southern rock band called Amadeus. The story played up the fact that the lead singer, TJ Russell, claimed to be the illegitimate son of rock and roll pioneer Teddy Boyette. Mainstream print media also picked it up. Soon after, the phone in the Rabinowitz home started ringing off the hook.

Joseph issued a straightforward and honest statement to those members of the press he trusted to give him a fair shake, "I have definite misgivings about this young man's claim. To my knowledge there is no proof to what he is saying. And until he is able to provide such proof I'd have to say I can't give any credence to his story." For those known to misquote him or take his words out of context, he gave a curt but courteous, "No comment."

Artie Franklin's publicity people were eager to engage in a media duel and quickly released the one piece of evidence TJ believed would settle the debate, a hand written letter sent to his mother by Cap Stewart.

> Dee:
>
> I should not at all be surprised to get something like this from you. I told Teddy you was a troublemaker and this just shows I was right.
> I hope you realize you got no proof to back up this ridiculous story you're spouting and I got no real reason to even respond.
> But on the off chance it is true I'll agree to send you some cash from time to time.
> I got no intention of ever letting on to Teddy any of this bull crap and I warn you strongly that if you ever try to contact him directly or I see or hear about any of this coming out in public, you'll have a heap of hurt brung down on you by Teddy's New York lawyers.
> Let this be the last of it! You hear?
>
> Cap Stewart

Joseph could only imagine the embarrassment young Mr. Russell felt to have such a letter printed in public. The scathing portrayal of his mother by Cap Stewart must be painful to say the least.

While Joseph dealt with this, it fell to Leo Klein to put together the packaging phase of Teddy's box set. The finished product consisted of five vinyl LP records or three cassette tapes. Appropriately sized printed material came in the form of a booklet. It contained the background material for each cut, the date of the original recording and those present. Select photographs from company files were used. The black and white picture on the cover of the set was taken by Janet on the observation deck of the Empire State Building during Teddy's first days in New York.

As always, Leo's meticulous work impressed Joseph.

"It all sounds terrific Leo. I can't wait to see it," Joseph said into the phone.

"It's going to *be* terrific as well, my friend." Then, after a pause, "This business with this TJ person…it's settled?"

"I'm not sure it'll ever be settled. I just want it to go away."

"Teddy was no angel Joseph. I can remember times…"

Joseph cut him off. "He was a young man, out on the road, lonely. Of course there were times, Cap was always there to take care of things. But…a son?"

🎵🎵🎵🎵🎵

TJ Russell never liked the name of his band Amadeus. In fact, he hated it. But that was already the name of the group when TJ came along, so there was nothing he could do about it.

"Wolfgang Amadeus Mozart, a seventeenth century composer of classical music, that's where it come from," Cam, short for Cameron Pierson, the band's founder told him. TJ came across the band on a visit to McGinty's Bar and Barbecue, a roadside joint near Fort Smith, Arkansas. He liked the sound the four member band put out and decided to have a talk with Pierson. After introducing himself as an out of work guitar player, he asked Cam who played a Hammond B-3 organ about the band and its name. "My folks were big on the classics. My mom still teaches music at the high school I went to. What do you think?"

"You got a great sound, especially with that B-3, you sure play the hell outta that thing. The other guys are okay," TJ offered.

Pierson laughed. "Thanks, it's not exactly what you call portable though." The console resembled a large piece of furniture rather than a musical instrument. It weighed in at 425 pounds and stood four feet square, not including the

Leslie tone cabinet containing the Rotosonic C speakers that accompanied it. It was too large for the small stage in the restaurant, so it was placed perpendicular to it. Three other musicians made up the rest of the band. The drummer and guitarist were school chums of Pierson's. A tall thin German-born blonde guy named Gunnar Baden played bass guitar and sang.

"Gunnar is the weak link, I know," Pierson explained. "He's pretty, which is good cause he's out front and attracts the chicks. But, he doesn't have a powerful enough voice, too whiney for my tastes. You looking for work?"

"Yeah, but I ain't lookin to do anybody out of their steady gig."

"Hey, at this point in time I gotta do what I think is best for the band. Why don't you hang around after our last set and you and me can jam for a bit."

"Okay."

McGinty's shut its doors at midnight, an hour after the kitchen closed. TJ and Cam Pierson were alone with the exception of the clean-up crew. Pierson offered him the use of an Epiphone guitar, which had great neck action. TJ sat on the edge of the stage next to the Hammond organ's bench.

"What's your pleasure?" Cam asked.

"'Sweet Home Alabama?'"

"Great tune."

The song, a top ten hit for the southern rock band Lynyrd Skynyrd, featured a raucous guitar riff intro and two long solos between verses. TJ nailed the intro. He sang without a microphone, loud enough for Cam to hear him. They jammed through the first solo and were coming out of the second when Pierson suddenly stopped playing.

"Let's take that second solo again," he told Russell.

This time, knowing exactly how TJ would play, Cam fashioned keyboard fills that made it sound more like the recorded version. They smiled when they finished.

"Better?" Cam asked.

TJ nodded, "Fantastic."

"We finish up this gig here next weekend. After that, it'll take a couple of days for me to send Gunnar packing and break the news to Tyler that I want him to switch over to bass guitar. After that, you and me need to spend some time together. I got a stack of original material I never showed these guys because I felt sure they couldn't handle it. I think *you* can. Interested?"

"Yeah I am, only…there's something you need to know about me."

The information TJ conveyed to him remained a secret between the two of them for the first year after TJ joined the band. Pierson's original material was golden. Between them, the two men put together more than two dozen songs they added to the band's repertoire. Amadeus become a solid performing band with a strong fan base.

When Cam learned about the upcoming auction of Teddy Boyette's memorabilia and possessions, he convinced TJ it was time to go public about his connection to the singer. They contacted Artie Franklin at Myriad Records and made their pitch to the record executive. Franklin took it from there. His label was in financial trouble and badly needed a new artist to revive interest. A talented new band like Amadeus, along with TJ's claim – true or not – seemed worth the risk.

Timing was perfect, in that it coincided with the auction. They plotted the scenario of pinching Chanticleer's Senorita down to the last detail including the two weeks spent seducing the young accomplice Renni Granger to help in the charade.

The confrontation and conversation with Joseph Rabinowitz was the icing on the cake. Although it was not as satisfying as TJ imagined it would be.

Amadeus signed a two-year contract with Myriad Records. The chemistry between TJ and Cam Pierson was a perfect fit. Pierson wrote the words and music to the songs. TJ added some strong guitar riffs and fills. It seemed like a fair deal that TJ be given co-arranger credit on the record label. The vocals were all TJ. His powerful, bluesy voice was out front on every song, with background vocals provided by the rest of the group.

Weeks after the publicity surrounding Cap Stewart's letter to TJ's mother played itself out, the group's first single "Riverboat Rambler" was released. The song rose steadily on the *Billboard* chart before stalling at number three and then began to slide. It was surpassed by the release of Teddy Boyette's re-mixed version of "Within a Wooded Chapel." The song became a posthumous number one hit sixteen years after the singer's death.

Chapter Sixteen:
"That's Where the Happy People Go"

In 1976, Americans celebrated the bicentennial anniversary of the signing of the Declaration of Independence. Many special events were planned nationwide. The US Treasury issued new designs for the quarter, half dollar and silver dollar. The two-dollar bill was re-introduced with a new reverse side depicting the signing of the historic document. Mailboxes and fire hydrants were painted red, white and blue.

The main focus would be the July 4th weekend. All the television networks planned specials. In New York Harbor, a fleet of more than sixteen international tall ships put on a nautical parade called "Operation Sail." Fireworks displays dominated the night sky all across the country.

At about this same time, a new music genre was about to explode on the scene. Disco, a form of dance music, permeated the scene in clubs of the same name. At first, discos played host to the African American, psychedelic and gay communities. But as the craze caught on, mainstream patrons from a wide range of age and ethnic groups came out in great numbers.

Discos were dimly lit, often illuminated by beams of colored light reflected off huge silver disco balls suspended from the ceiling. Large wooden dance floors offered plenty of room for free form dancing. Recorded music played through huge speakers and sound systems. DJ's used multiple turntables to keep the music going through long sets testing the limits and abilities of the dancers.

The genre sparked its own style of fashion. Men wore tight flared bell-bottom trousers, multi-colored shirts with butterfly style collars or polyester knit leisure suits, vests and patent leather shoes with wide heels. Women were quite creative in their club wear. Some had big hair ranging from Afros to wavy tresses framing their face. Their dresses ranged from swirl mini styles to mid-length pleated skirts made of silver or gold lamé. High spiked heels or leather disco boots adorned their feet.

The music itself derived its influences from soul or Latin music. Loud vocals backed by a thundering percussion and a syncopated bass line mixed with lush instrumental tracks featuring horns, strings and sometimes a flute replacing lead guitar. The disco era brought forth many great artists and performers. A group from Philadelphia, called the Trammps, recorded a song whose lyrics exemplified the joy of the disco scene, "Down at the Disco...that's where the happy people go."

Donna Summer, a smooth voiced singer arrived on the scene with a song called "Love to Love You Baby." Long stretches of reverberated moaning and groaning sounded very much like a woman in the throes of sexual ecstasy.

Before long, local discos and dance clubs sprung up in all five boroughs of New York City. They offered great music and dancing to common folks unable to attend the more trendy nightspots in Manhattan like CBGB's, Max's Kansas City or the super swanky Studio 54.

As is usually the case, a genre cannot be said to succeed until it is parodied in some way. Rick Dees, a disc jockey at radio station WMPS-AM in Memphis, wrote a tune based on a dance song called "The Duck" recorded by Jackie Lee in 1965. Dees called his effort "Disco Duck" and used a Donald Duck sound-alike voice provided by a friend of his, Ken Pruitt. The song was #1 on the *Billboard* chart for one week and remained in the top ten for ten more.

♪ ♪ ♪ ♪ ♪

Bobby Vitale came off the stage after the last set of the night at the Starship Room of the Stardust Hotel in Las Vegas. He was almost tackled by an older female fan who appeared out of nowhere. The woman wore a tight fitting dress that clung to her stout figure. She put him in a tight bear hug and planted a big sloppy kiss on his mouth, smearing her dark red lipstick.

"Oh, Bobby, I've loved your music for so many years. I absolutely adore all you guys." She tried to kiss him again, but he managed to free himself from her grip.

"Yeah, yeah, thanks a lot."

The woman pressed a small piece of folded paper into his hand before he made his way through a thick curtain leading to the backstage area. He put the note in his pocket. No need to look at it, a name and room number, phone number, or something like that.

His next encounter was much more pleasurable. Cassie, a tall long-legged cocktail waitress with red hair, met him in the back corridor with his usual after show drink. She smiled as she handed him a double Dewar's Scotch and water.

"Thanks sweetie," he said retrieving a five-dollar bill from his pocket and handing it to her.

"My pleasure good looking," Cassie answered adding a wink before she walked away.

Bobby pushed his way into the dressing area used by singers and musicians alike. The three younger men who performed as the other Du-Kanes were already in their street clothes. Two of them brushed past him with hardly a word or gesture of farewell. The third, a good-looking kid named Alex who sang Johnny's parts, had something to say.

"I'm off to that two week gig in Reno. Sammy Balto will be filling in for me most nights."

"Whoa, whoa. Whaddaya mean *most nights*?" Bobby asked.

"Yeah, I told ya he's got a couple of prior commitments he's gotta honor."

"What am I supposed to do on the nights he can't make it?" Bobby was concerned, Alex didn't seem to care.

"You'll work it out. You can always call Desmond. I gotta go. See ya in two weeks." Alex quickly squirted his way through the curtain.

Now, alone, Bobby was angry. The attitude Alex and many of these replacement singers had these days was always the same. They performed with his oldies group, but the minute something better came along they were gone. He used the singer Desmond before, though he was barely adequate. His frequent mistakes on stage were embarrassing.

Bobby took a seat at a dressing table set up along one wall and looked at his reflection in a mirror. In the last couple of years, he'd gone gray but still had a full head of hair. No lines, no wrinkles on his face and amazingly, no bags under his clear brown eyes. As he sipped his cocktail, the aroma of an expensive Cuban cigar wafted his way. That meant Ira Weiss, assistant entertainment director for the Stardust Hotel was about to make his patented grand entrance. After doing so, he extended his hand to Bobby.

"What's happening kiddo?"

"I'm doing good Ira."

After shaking hands, Weiss took a seat next to him. If his cigar was expensive, his wardrobe was not. He wore a rumpled jacket with a black paisley design. His ruffled white shirt bore a coffee stain across the front and a black tie was loosened at his open collar. He had a round face and belly and wore tinted glasses even when inside.

"I'm here to tell you we aren't renewing your contract after this month, sorry." His Midwestern accent screamed Chicago and his voice was coarse and raspy.

"C'mon Ira," Bobby pleaded, "We've had this conversation before."

"Yeah, yeah, I know. But this time it's for real. This doo-wop shit just ain't cuttin it no more."

"Can't you talk to someone?"

"Talking is done. Three weeks and you're out. Upstairs management wants to bring in something makes people wanna get up and dance."

"What do they think is gonna make this crowd *dance*?"

Ira waved a hand in Bobby's face and shook his head. "Some kinda disco shit I suppose. What do I know?"

Doo-wop shit and disco shit, Bobby guessed Ira thought all music was shit.

Ira continued, "I know you a long time Bobby, you're gonna land on your feet. Take a few weeks off, re-work the act and bring it more up-to-date. Maybe put a couple chicks out front. Tits and ass, that always works in this town, you oughtta know that." When Bobby didn't answer Ira stood up. "Or, you could go back to dealing blackjack. You had to make more money at that than doin this shit." He coughed up a sarcastic laugh before slapping the singer on the back on his way out.

Bobby sat there thinking all the way back to sixty-nine when *Bobby Vitale's Du-Kanes* first began performing in Las Vegas. The group headlined the biggest and best showrooms on the Strip, the Sands, the Dunes and the Sahara. They followed Elvis Presley into the International Hotel and played to packed houses every night.

Eventually, the size of the venues and the crowds began to dwindle. For a time they opened for top acts like Liberace, Tony Bennett and comedian Don Rickles. They soon found themselves banished to smaller lounges and smaller fees. That made it difficult to keep reliable singers in the group. Getting fired from this dump was like falling off the bottom rung of a ladder.

You can always go back to dealing blackjack.

Ira's insulting comment echoed in his brain. He knew he couldn't go back, not anymore. Bobby reached into his pocket and removed the folded cocktail napkin that annoying fan slipped him earlier, "Gladys Room 1035." Beneath the short message, a splotchy imprint of her lipstick implied a hopeful declaration.

"Why not?" he muttered.

♫ ♫ ♫ ♫ ♫

The voice of Don Imus, the morning DJ on WNBC radio, was the first thing Johnny Seracino heard every day when the clock radio on his side of the bed went off at 7am.

Like Alan Freed before him, Imus moved to New York from Cleveland, Ohio. There he gained the reputation of being a radical personality. A radio station in California once fired him for calling a local fast food restaurant and ordering 1,200 hamburgers to go. His New York show, *Imusinamorning*, mixed the station's Top-40 record rotation with comedy skits involving characters of Imus' own creation.

On this particular morning, Imus portrayed his favorite character, a Deep South evangelist named Billy Sol Hargus who was always out to raise funds for his "First Church of the Gooey Death and Discount House of Worship."

"Just send one twenty-nine ninety-nine plus tax and shipping and handling to Billy Sol Hargus at this radio station and you'll receive our exclusive Stable in Bethlehem Christmas Lawn Set, a six foot tall balsa wood mock-up of the place where Christ was born. You'll also receive six Madame Tussauds quality full-size wax images of two shepherds, two sheep, Joseph and the Virgin Mary. Act now and you'll also receive our Star of Bethlehem Rotating Disco Ball, which can easily be affixed to the top of the structure and usable year-round for your indoor disco dance parties. Act now, supplies are limited…baby Jesus not included."

Johnny smiled as he clicked off the radio.

"That guy is such an asshole," Barbara said as she stirred beside him.

"I think he's pretty funny."

"Ughhh," his wife groaned.

She was gone from the bed by the time Johnny came back to the bedroom after his shower. He got dressed and went downstairs. He passed his son Stevie as he entered the kitchen.

"You have to take the truck to the yard today," he told

his son. Stevie, now eighteen, worked with him at the Morris Park Lumber Yard. "I'm having breakfast with Joe Rabin at the Thruway Diner."

"Okay," was all Stevie said as he kept walking.

"You have time for coffee?" Barbara asked.

"Just a quick cup."

"Does Joe have more shows for you?"

"He didn't say. It would be nice though."

"You're not kidding."

The American economy was going through difficult times. Added income was always welcome.

♫ ♫ ♫ ♫ ♫

The Thruway Diner on Boston Post Road was a popular eating and meeting spot located just off the New Rochelle Exit of I-95, something of a midway point for Johnny in the Bronx and Joseph in Rye.

When Johnny arrived, Joseph was sitting at a booth sipping coffee. Johnny ordered french toast with bacon. They exchanged pleasantries before Joseph got to the reason for their meeting. He wanted the Du-Kanes to record a new album updating all their biggest hits. "I can't guarantee you'll get a new hit record out of it like we had with Teddy, but I think a new LP and cassette would sell great at shows."

"Yeah, that sounds really great Joe." Johnny's lit up expression showed his excitement.

"We'll re-record all the tracks, make some improvements...do some things we weren't able to do years back."

"Shit, I can't wait to tell Kenny and Frankie." Kenny Liebermann was another original Du-Kane, and Frankie had been with the group since the first re-union show in sixty-nine. "And Bobby? Bobby will fly back here without a friggin plane."

Joseph's tone became serious. "I wasn't going to use

Bobby on this project Johnny."

Johnny sat back hard in the booth showing his concern. "How can you not use Bobby?"

"He's been cooperative by coming back for our two big shows every year and I appreciate that. But, he's also still performing out in Vegas with this group he put together calling himself the Du-Kanes doing the songs…"

"Why shouldn't he use the name? He's the one who came up with it for Chrissake."

"It's a trademark issue, a contractual thing…"

"Small print?" Johnny interrupted him. "Bobby wasn't ever much for the small print, Joseph, none of us were. We just signed whatever you put in front of us."

Johnny was right. The Du-Kanes, like so many other younger artists, trusted their record companies and managers. They often committed to long term contracts without really understanding how much they would be paid or what the working conditions would be like. Though the acts who signed with Joseph's Chanticleer Record label were always treated fairly, there was never a reason for question or concern…until now.

Joseph sought to defend himself. "Look Johnny, I know how you feel, but…"

Johnny cut him off a second time, "I can remember you coming to my house on a cold winter night a few years back, asking me to do you a favor and fly out to Vegas and get Bobby to come back and do a show. That seems to have worked out pretty good for you."

Joseph understood perfectly. "You calling in a marker Johnny?"

"Just think of it as *me* asking *you* for a favor this time."

After some thought Joseph relented, "Okay, go ahead and call Bobby. If he's interested, we'll get you into the studio right after the holidays."

Gerald Ford was a true anomaly in American politics. He served as President and Vice-President of the United States without any American citizen ever casting a vote for him.

In 1964, Ford served as a congressman from his home state of Michigan. Republican party leaders approached him to run for the office of House Minority Leader. Ford won a closely contested race. He began to publically criticize the Johnson administration's handling of the Vietnam War. One speech so outraged Johnson that it caused the president to comment, "Jerry Ford's been playing too much football without a helmet."

With Richard Nixon's election as President in 1968, Ford adapted well to his role as a loyal party member.

That summer Vice-President Spiro Agnew came under investigation by the Attorney General's Office on charges of extortion, tax fraud, bribery and conspiracy dating back to 1967 when he was governor of Maryland. After he was formally charged he pled "no contest" thus avoiding an embarrassing trial. One of the conditions of the agreement included his resignation as vice-president.

Gerald Ford was nominated to replace Agnew and his confirmation overwhelmingly approved.

When Richard Nixon resigned in disgrace in August of 1974, Ford was appointed the 38th President of the United States.

A month later, Ford issued a conditional amnesty for Vietnam War draft dodgers who fled the country. Then, he shocked the nation and the world by issuing a proclamation giving Richard Nixon a complete and unconditional pardon for any crimes he may have committed as president. Many saw this as an admission that Nixon was indeed guilty for his part in the Watergate conspiracy. *The New York Times* called Ford's action, "A profoundly unwise, divisive and unjust act that destroyed Ford's credibility as a man of judgment."

This coupled with the fact that during Ford's tenure the

country suffered through the worst recession since the Great Depression, were seen as the main reasons why Ford narrowly defeated Ronald Reagan, the actor and former governor of California for the Republican presidential nomination. Ford lost the General election making Democrat Jimmy Carter, the 39th President of the United States.

Chapter Seventeen:
".44"

New York City sweltered during the summer of 1977. Record high temperatures and breath draining humidity took its toll on citizens. Emergency rooms experienced overcrowding as senior citizens sought relief from severe respiratory problems. City officials rounded up the homeless and put them into shelters. To make matters worse, on the evening of July13, a series of lightning strikes caused the entire Consolidated Edison electrical system to shut down thrusting almost all of New York City into darkness. Unlike the blackout of 1965, this time widespread looting, violence and arson caused major havoc.

Then, of course, there was the Son of Sam.

Beginning in July 1976, seven shooting incidents with similar circumstances occurred in the boroughs of the Bronx and Queens. All took place overnight in residential neighborhoods. The victims were mostly couples often shot in their parked cars. All the females had short brown hair. Witnesses described the shooter as a short chubby white male with fair complexion, in his twenties or thirties, driving a yellow car. In all, five people were killed and six others wounded. The crimes appeared random and unconnected until New York City Mayor Abe Beame held a press conference in March 1977. He announced that ballistics showed that the weapon used in all the crimes was a .44 caliber Charter Arms Bulldog revolver. A serial killer was on the loose.

The press initially labeled him the .44 Caliber Killer. After the fatal shooting of a Bronx couple in July, police found a letter at the crime scene addressed to the NYPD. The killer called himself the Son of Sam. The new name stuck and the manhunt continued.

♪ ♪ ♪ ♪ ♪

Jimmy Stannic came to hate his job with the Transit Authority. For nineteen years he remained in the same position as a track maintenance worker. He tried several times to advance through the ranks. Jimmy took the test for motorman and conductor several times but failed on each occasion. It was difficult for him to grasp any new systems or procedures that came along improving the subway. He was written up several times for poor workmanship. The only good thing about the job was that nobody there called him Geep.

His co-workers had other names for him. "Kid" worked for a few years. Little Stannic replaced that until Jimmy's father died in 1970 from emphysema. The circumstances of his father's death fueled Jimmy's paranoia of gasping for air and suffering a similar fate.

It wasn't *just* his job. Life in general became a journey of almost continuous disappointment and failure. He didn't have many friends, except for a group of guys at work with whom he went out on Friday nights. They hung out in bars like the Tender Trap, or Joe and Joe's on Bruckner Boulevard.

His love life bordered on abysmal. Jimmy never had a steady girlfriend. At times he went on blind dates with women introduced to him by others. They seldom led to anything of a lasting nature and rarely involved sex. Instead, he masturbated or procured the services of prostitutes roaming the deserted streets of the nearby Hunt's Point Terminal Market after business hours.

The fact was Jimmy still pined after Barbara Seracino. Jimmy continued to follow the Du-Kanes whenever they appeared in the tri-state area, if for no other reason, than to run into Barbara and perhaps say hello and chat.

There *was* another woman, a waitress named Annette who worked at the Castle Hill Diner, near the subway yard where he reported for work. She was a cute young brunette who always smiled as she served him breakfast from across the counter. He learned that she lived on nearby Allerton Avenue, had a boyfriend and loved to dance.

"Do you dance?" she asked him one morning. "Can you do the hustle?"

Jimmy shook his head.

The Hustle was the latest line dance craze in discos. It was based on the song of the same name recorded by Van McCoy & the Soul City Symphony, which topped the *Billboard* chart in the summer of 1975. Since then, newer variations of the dance had been introduced. The latest version, and the one Annette wanted to learn, was called the Bus Stop.

"I suppose I could learn," Jimmy added.

This gave Annette an idea. She looked upon him as something of a simpleton, weak, harmless, someone easy to control and handle if he ever came on to her. Her boyfriend, Peter, wanted no part of what he called "Guido disco bullshit." Jimmy might just be the person she could use.

"There's a disco up in New Rochelle called Li'l Abners," she told Jimmy placing a hot coffee refill in front of him. "Every Tuesday night they give dance lessons. I'm thinking of going, but I don't want to go alone because of this Son of Sam creep."

"Maybe I could take you there?" Jimmy eagerly volunteered.

"Well, I don't know about that. But I *could* meet you there every week."

"Yeah sure. I'd love to do that."

They made plans to meet outside the club at seven o'clock the following Tuesday night. Jimmy was sure Annette liked him, at least well enough to be her dance partner. It meant he'd have to learn the hustle, but really, how hard could that be? The important thing now was that for the first time in a long time, he had someone new to fantasize about when he played with himself in bed at night.

♫♫♫♫♫

Jimmy found the atmosphere inside L'il Abners extremely exciting. The colored lights flashing all around, the pulsating beat of the music, the bodies of young men and women spinning and swirling on the crowded dance floor was something he had never seen before.

A full service bar with stools stood just inside the entryway. There was a series of vinyl-upholstered booths forming a perimeter around the dance floor. A loft on the club's second floor provided patrons a bird's eye view of the crowd below. This created a darkened alcove on the main level. Several rows of tables and chairs provided the perfect make-out spot.

The dance lessons began a full hour the before the club opened for business and cost ten dollars per couple. Jimmy paid for their full four-week enrollment. Things went fine the first week, except for the way Jimmy dressed. He showed up wearing a very loud multi-colored silk shirt, a pair of lime green flared-legged pants and suede desert boots he thought would be comfortable to dance in.

Annette, on the other hand looked very pretty. Her hair was styled high on her head and her make-up perfectly applied. She wore a calf length dress with a flowing skirt and high heels. There were ten or twelve other couples taking lessons that night. Midway through, Jimmy realized dancing wasn't going to be as easy as he thought.

Learning the Hustle involved memorizing a series of steps and moves to the right and left. There were spins, twirls and turns that would sometimes cause Jimmy to bump into one of the couples, or even worse, step on Annette's foot.

Things were no better after the second week's lesson.

On the Tuesday morning of the third week, Annette didn't greet Jimmy with a smile when he came into the diner. She knew he wouldn't like what she had to tell him, but she had the perfect excuse. "Did you see? The Son of Sam shot another couple Sunday night. He followed them from a disco out in Queens."

"Yeah, sure I saw it. It's all over the news."

She poured him a cup of coffee. "Well, my boyfriend says its way too dangerous to go out to any discos, so I can't go for dance lessons anymore."

Her news hit him hard. Jimmy struggled for a solution. "You could dye your hair blonde so you won't look like any of his victims. I hear lots of girls are doing that."

"Yeah I know, but my boyfriend would never let me do that. He likes my hair the way it is." She became firm with him. "Look, I just can't go anymore. I'm sorry."

Jimmy didn't believe her. It sounded like a cockeyed excuse and he thought, *you're just another fucked up bitch.*

♫♫♫♫♫

The fact that Annette backed out wouldn't deter him from going to L'il Abners. He had forty bucks invested and even if he didn't have a partner for the lesson he was determined to be there anyway.

Because of the recent shootings, many patrons stayed away. The place was only half full. Police sketches of the Son of Sam culled from eyewitness and surviving victim's accounts, hung on walls, behind the bar and in both the men's and women's restrooms. In spite of that, those on the dance floor still partied hard. After ordering his usual drink, a rum and Coke, Jimmy leaned against a pole beneath the alcove partition on the main floor.

His gaze fell upon two blonde girls dancing close to where he stood. The song "Don't Leave Me This Way" blared through the speakers. One of the girls made eye contact and then quickly looked away. Jimmy took that to mean she might be interested. The song segued into a re-mix disco version of an old Crystals' song, "Da Doo Ron Ron." Partway through, the girls left the dance floor. Jimmy flashed a big friendly smile at them but they simply looked at one another, chuckled and continued on.

Filled with rejection he melted into the shadowy darkness of the alcove. He was about to mutter some choice curse words when a soft voice spoke from behind him, "Cute, aren't they?"

Though startled, Jimmy didn't turn around. "Yeah, I guess. Kinda stuck-up though."

"Too good for guys like us, huh?"

"Yeah, like their shit don't stink," Jimmy replied.

"These places are full of broads like that. I like the girls from Queens. They are the prettiest of all."

Jimmy turned his head to the side, but only caught the silhouette of someone shorter than him. "Are you from around here?" Jimmy asked.

What followed frightened Jimmy to the very depth of his soul.

"I am from the gutters of New York City. The gutters filled with dog manure, vomit, stale wine, urine and blood." The voice spoke in a quiet even tone with no hint of the anger his words portrayed. "These cows proffer their braless breasts like Salome bargaining for the head of John the Baptist. They treat us with such contempt and disdain unaware of the proximity of death, for I am the Son of Sam. I have more work to do. My drunken father demands that I hunt, commands me to go out and kill. I love to kill. And I will kill again. What will you have for July 29th?"

Jimmy felt his heart pound inside his chest. If this guy really was the Son of Sam he could start shooting at any minute. Despite white hot flashes of danger, he managed to start walking without so much as a glance in either direction. He didn't stop until he was out in the street and safely in his car.

The headlines the next day did not speak of murder and mayhem. Jimmy now thought that the menacing voice in the darkness was just some drunken asshole spouting off. Still, what if the guy really *was* the Son of Sam checking out the disco for his next attack? And the date, that specific date...*what have you got for July 29th?* He could go to the police but they probably wouldn't believe him, or it might even cast suspicion on himself. No, that was no good, but he *had* to do something.

A fantasy formed in his mind and gained momentum as weeks passed. What if he went to L'il Abners on the night of the 29th and captured the serial killer. He'd be famous, a hero. *Jimmy Stannic, the man who captured the Son of Sam.*

That would show them. That would show all of them, the assholes in his neighborhood who called him Geep when he was a kid. Barbara Seracino, she'd see that he was more important than that stupid singer she married. He'd walk around the Transit Authority yard with his head held high accepting pats on the back from all his co-workers. And finally, *he'd give that bitch Annette something to think about.*

Catching a killer would be dangerous work. He needed to be prepared.

♫ ♫ ♫ ♫ ♫

It was 2am when Jimmy guided his 1970 Plymouth Duster off Barrett Street and onto Oak Point Avenue toward the Hunts Point Terminal Market. By day, the area was crowded with tractor-trailer trucks and commercial vehicles. They picked up and delivered fresh fruit and vegetables for distribution to supermarkets and small neighborhood stores all over the city.

During the overnight hours, darker activities took place. Drug deals were conducted in many a shadowy doorway. Dozens of prostitutes lined both sides of the street in varying degrees of undress. Jimmy was no stranger to the ladies of the night and one of them in particular, a heavyset black woman named Jasmine.

Jasmine had a light mocha complexion. Her face was badly blemished with dark circles around her eyes making it impossible to guess her age. She wore her hair in Jheri curls, a glossy loose curled look. Once, when Jasmine had her head down in his crotch, Jimmy made the mistake of running his hand through her hair rendering it sticky and messy. He had to reach back and wipe it clean on the car's upholstery. She maintained a regular spot outside the A-1 Auto Repair Shop propped against one of two big red garage doors now shut and locked tight.

The hooker moved to the curb as soon as the Duster pulled up. She jumped in, closed the door behind her and immediately lowered the red halter top she wore to expose her large breasts. She leaned over and thrust one directly in Jimmy's face. "What's it gonna be for you tonight sugah hand job or blow job?"

Jimmy pushed her back a bit and waved a folded one-hundred dollar bill in his face. "Nah, none of that shit tonight."

Jasmine gave him a stern look. "Now look here, I told you time and again, you and me ain't never gonna do no penetratin intercourse."

"No, no this money's not for sex."

"What then?"

"I want you to get me a gun."

"A gun? What the fuck you need a gun for?"

Jimmy had a well-rehearsed lie. "It's dangerous around here, last time I almost got mugged by a couple of drug dealers."

"Thas cause you was prolly sniffin round the Point for a stray piece of trim. Jasmine got the finest piece of ass you're gonna find round here. No need to look elsewhere."

"I know that baby. I'm just looking for a different kind of piece now, a forty-four."

Jimmy's attempt at humor made her chuckle. "A forty-four, eh…just like that Son of Sam motherfucker?"

"That's right, just like the Son of Sam. Can you help me?"

"You got another one of those Ben Franklins?"

"Maybe," he expected some kind of negotiation. "Why?"

"Might be I know someone can help you out. One Franklin won't cut it, but two might do the trick and leave over a nice chunk of change for ole Jasmine. Call it a finder's fee."

"Okay, two hundred."

"But we gotta go to the Soundview Projects to get it and we gotta go now."

On hearing this, Jimmy became concerned. If he wanted the handgun, he'd have to risk it.

Budget cuts saw some city housing projects deteriorate to the point that a rather unsavory element inhabited some buildings. The development on Soundview Avenue was one of them. The red brick buildings were covered with graffiti or in need of repair, the grounds littered with garbage and overgrown with weeds.

Jasmine brought Jimmy to the apartment of a rather scary and unpleasant black man she identified only as Peachie.

"Two hundred dollas ain't gonna git you much," Peachie managed to spew out of a mouth missing several front teeth. "Specially no forty-four – thas a expensive piece of hardware."

"What *will* it get me?" Jimmy asked.

"I can let you have this here Smith and Wesson thirty-eight. The grip is broke but the business end of it works just fine. I'll even throw in a box of ammo."

"C'mon now Peachie," Jasmine interrupted, perhaps seeing her finder's fee evaporating. "I told you Jimmy was a good friend of mine. Don't you be takin advantage now."

"All right, don't jump down my throat. I'll give your

friend here the whole package for one-fifty, how dat?"

Everyone went home happy.

🎵🎵🎵🎵🎵

On the evening of July 29th Jimmy got to the disco early. Again, the crowd fell well below normal size. He checked out the bar area paying special attention to any single guys there. Of course, Jimmy wouldn't recognize the man who spoke to him in the shadows, but he looked for anyone stalking the girls or acting suspicious. He went upstairs to the balcony. His eyes scanned the dance floor below, but found nothing out of the ordinary there, just young people dancing in a synchronized line like mindless robots to a song called "Shake Your Booty."

Even in the alcove beneath the overhang nothing sinister transpired among the couples beyond some heavy necking and petting.

Closing time came and went without incident. Jimmy seethed with anger at wasting his time standing vigil at the disco. He sat in his car for a while banging on the dashboard cursing his own stupidity, feeling cheated out of his hero opportunity.

🎵🎵🎵🎵🎵

Two days later, the Son of Sam struck again, this time in the Gravesend Beach area of Brooklyn. He shot a young couple making out in their car. The woman died of her wounds and her male companion was seriously injured. Unlike the prior crimes, this shooting produced a good many eyewitness accounts. Police put together a more accurate description of the killer. They were looking for a man, 25 to 30 years old, of average height, shaggy hair, with a round face and dark eyes. Some claimed to have seen the killer in a yellow Volkswagen Beetle.

After reading these accounts in a newspaper, a Brooklyn woman living near the crime scene called police. She reported seeing a man answering to that description remove a parking ticket from the windshield of his yellow Ford Galaxy. The car was parked too close to a fire hydrant.

NYPD obtained a list of all registered yellow Ford Galaxies in the tri-state area with the intent of checking them all. Police identified one such vehicle registered to a twenty-three year old postal worker named David Berkowitz. Berkowitz lived on Pine Street in Yonkers. Bronx detectives accompanied Yonkers police to the address. They found the Ford Galaxy parked on the street. A visual inspection revealed a partially covered rifle in the back seat. Police staked out the area. At 10pm, a man emerged from the building carrying a paper bag. When he got into the Ford Galaxy, the cops moved in and removed him from the vehicle. They found a .44 caliber Bulldog revolver in the paper bag. Confirming the man's identity as David Berkowitz, they arrested him.

Berkowitz commented calmly, "You got me. What took you so long?"

♫♫♫♫♫

In the days that followed the arrest, Jimmy Stannic along with thousands of others, watched as details of the killer's life became public. Berkowitz appeared to be a pathetic little man. Photographed in the back seat of the police car that transported him, he gawked at the cameras flashing from every direction. He seemed confused by the questions hurled at him from reporters sticking microphones and notebooks in his face.

Jimmy fantasized about a plan to go to the police precinct where Berkowitz was being held. There he would spring forward and shoot him, just the way Jack Ruby did in 1963 when he killed President John F. Kennedy's assassin Lee Harvey Oswald. But, since he had no desire to go to prison, he abandoned the idea. He put his .38 away in the secret lock box where he kept his collection of porn magazines. He felt certain his chance for fame would still one day come along.

Chapter Eighteen
"The King is Dead…"

Since his triumphant return to Las Vegas in July 1969, Elvis Presley enjoyed a renewed popularity in both his recording and performing careers. He signed a lucrative and long term contract to play Vegas twice a year. In addition, he committed to a strenuous series of tour dates in arena venues all across the country. On stage, Elvis wore tight-fitting jumpsuits studded with sequins and expensive jewels weighing as much as thirty pounds. His act reached a level of spectacular showmanship. The pace was grueling and took its effect on his health.

He suffered from a wide variety of ailments including back pain, insomnia, high blood pressure and weight gain. Elvis hired a full-time personal physician, Doctor George Nichopoulos, whom everyone called Dr. Nick. He prescribed and dispensed an abundance of prescription drugs and kept a careful eye on his patient's condition. Despite this, Presley overdosed twice on barbiturates. Later, he slipped into a semi-coma from his addiction to Demerol.

His condition deteriorated after the divorce from his wife Priscilla, but Elvis refused to cut back on his workload. Between July 1973 and October 1976, he recorded enough content for six albums. However, frequent temper tantrums in the studio resulted in the destruction of valuable equipment, which caused him further injury and required more pain killing drugs.

His personal image soon became an issue. Performances were shortened, or in some instances canceled. In Rapid City, South Dakota Elvis appeared onstage with a puffy face and bloated body. One reviewer commented "…in that white jumpsuit of his he looked like ten pounds of sausage in a five pound bag." He forgot the words to "Are You Lonesome Tonight," but joked his way through it. He told the audience, "I'm gonna play guitar on this one…I only know three chords...I faked out a lot of people over the years." When he sang the Frank Sinatra tune "My Way," he held a piece of paper and literally read the lyrics from it.

Six weeks later, on August 16, 1977, he was at his mansion home Graceland preparing to fly out the next day for a performance in Maine. He and his girlfriend Ginger Alden rested in bed. Elvis got up and went to the bathroom.

"Don't fall asleep in there," Alden told the singer.

"I won't," he replied.

Alden dozed off and woke sometime later, alone in bed. She went to the bathroom and found Presley passed out on the floor. In a panic, she called downstairs to the office for help. One of the first to arrive was Joe Esposito, Elvis' longtime friend and confidant. He found the star face down and unresponsive in the plush carpeting. The singer had apparently fallen off the commode. Esposito called the office and instructed an employee to call 911 and contact Dr. Nick.

An ambulance and Nichopoulous arrived at Graceland, but were unable to revive Presley. He was transported to Baptist Memorial Hospital in Memphis. Sometime later, a spokesman announced to the crowd of reporters that Elvis Presley had died of a heart attack. He was forty-two years old.

Thousands of fans viewed his open casket. The funeral took place at Graceland. An estimated 80,000 people lined the route to watch as a procession of all white limousines drove from Graceland to the Forest Hill Cemetery. Elvis was buried alongside his mother, Gladys.

Weeks later, after an attempt was made to steal the singer's body, both caskets were exhumed and reburied in the Meditation Garden at Graceland.

Chapter Nineteen:
"Hello From the Children of Planet Earth"

On August 20th 1977, NASA launched a deep space probe called Voyager 2 from Space Launch Complex 41 at Cape Canaveral, Florida. Two weeks later a twin sister probe, Voyager 1, followed it into space. Traveling at different trajectories, it was their mission to observe and send back data on the planets Jupiter and Saturn. The probes would continue beyond our solar system in search of intelligent life. They would also carry a *Golden Record*, an audio chronicle of the history of life on earth, making the spacecraft a deep space time capsule.

The mission met with opposition on several fronts. The majority viewed it as a drain on finances in a time of severe budget cuts. Many religious leaders thought it a dangerous folly, a threat to the very basic ideology of evolution by even hinting that intelligent life existed elsewhere. It didn't help when NASA chose noted astronomer and astrophysicist Carl Sagan, an admitted agnostic, as chairman of the committee to select the contents of the gold plated audio-visual disc accompanying the spacecraft on its journey.

United Nations Secretary-General Kurt Waldheim and US President Jimmy Carter provided written statements placed within the capsule explaining the purpose of the mission. Carter's message read in part, "We cast this message into the cosmos... Of the 200 billion stars in the Milky Way galaxy, some, perhaps many, may have inhabited planets and space faring civilizations. If one such civilization intercepts Voyager and can understand these recorded contents, here is our message: 'We are trying to survive our time so we may live into yours. We hope someday, having solved the problems we face, to join a community of Galactic civilizations. This record represents our hope and our determination and our goodwill in a vast and awesome universe.'"

The Voyager's *Golden Record* contained 116 pictures representing life on earth. In the event that either of the probes did indeed encounter intelligent life in the far reaches of space, the discs would give extraterrestrials an insight to our civilization.

The committee gathered spoken greetings in 55 different languages. Sagan's six-year-old son, Nick, provided the voice for the English language greeting, "Hello from the children of planet Earth."

Another section was devoted to the "sounds of the earth" as diverse as thunder, wind, rain, surf, and a whale's song. A 90-minute collection of music from many different cultures and eras followed. This included a Pygmy girl's initiation song, a "Navajo Indian Night Chant," and classical works by composers Bach, Beethoven, Mozart and Stravinsky. Louis Armstrong and his Hot Seven Combo provided an example of American jazz called "Melancholy Blues." Blind Willie Johnson's R&B guitar lament "Dark Was the Night, Cold Was the Ground" was also included. Sagan sought to acquire the Beatles tune "Here Comes the Sun" from the *Abbey Road* album but their music publisher EMI denied him permission. Chuck Berry and his song "Johnny B. Goode" represented rock and roll on the *Golden Record*.

♫♫♫♫♫

Despite the fact that David Berkowitz was locked up in the Attica State Correctional Facility in upstate New York, serving a 365-year sentence as the Son of Sam killer, the disco music scene started to wane. The genre received a huge shot in the arm with the release of the motion picture *Saturday Night Fever*. The film starred John Travolta, already a teen icon for his role as the likeable delinquent Vinny Barbarino in the hit TV series *Welcome Back Kotter*. He portrayed a harder edged character in *Fever* named Tony Manero.

The film explored aspects of the life of a group of

Brooklyn young people, their culture, their disillusioned attitude toward the establishment, sexual mores and racial tensions. Centering around a Brooklyn disco called "2001 Odyssey" audiences were bombarded with images of the latest fashion, choreography and music.

Since 1967, the Bee Gees, brothers Barry, Robin and Maurice Gibb had a successful career highlighted by their tight three-part harmonies and Robin's strong vibrato vocals. They enjoyed a long string of successful baroque pop ballads. Creative differences caused Robin to leave the group. His brother Barry then developed a strong falsetto style of singing. The brothers soon reunited and moved to Florida where producer Robert Stigwood suggested they write upbeat tunes to take advantage of the nationwide disco dance craze. The success of the new material inspired the group to submit several demo tracks for the *Saturday Night Fever* soundtrack album. Five of the demos were chosen: "Stayin' Alive," "Night Fever," "More Than a Woman," "How Deep is Your Love," and "If I Can't Have You."

With the film's release in December 1977, *Saturday Night Fever* and its soundtrack album soared to unparalleled success.

♫♫♫♫♫

On Saturday April 28th 1978, the immensely popular NBC Television late night comedy series *Saturday Night Live* presented a sketch called "Next Week in Review." The piece featured series regulars Laraine Newman and Dan Ackroyd, along with guest host comedian Steve Martin. Newman, acting as moderator, interviewed psychics whose job it was to predict the headlines appearing on the cover of *Time* magazine the following week. Martin provided the set-up.

"A far off planet actually sent us a message last week. Next week, the government will reveal the content of the message."

By way of explanation, Ackroyd then talked about the launch of Voyager 1, the year before, the *Golden Record* and its contents. When he mentioned the music section, he wrapped up by saying "…everything from classical music to Chuck Berry."

"And you're saying that another civilization has found the tape?" Newman asked.

"Yes, they sent us a message which actually proves it," Martin replied. "It may be just four simple words but it is the first actual proof that other intelligent beings inhabit the universe."

"And what are those four words?" the moderator inquired.

"The four words that came to us from outer space, the four words that will appear on the cover of *Time* magazine next week are…" Martin then held up a prop copy of *Time* magazine and presented it to the camera as he delivered the punch line "send more Chuck Berry."

Chapter Twenty:
"Feel the Love"

In the years since leaving the singing group the Pixies at the height of their career to go solo, Evie Rhodes rose to superstar status. She was the glittering jewel of Malcolm Brown's South Side record label. Her popularity and success enabled Brown to move his entire operation from Chicago to Hollywood.

She won a Grammy for Best Performance by a Female Artist in 1970 with "Feel the Love," a haunting ballad written for her by the songwriting team of Nick Ashford and Valerie Simpson. The tune held the number one spot on the *Billboard* chart for three consecutive weeks. Her enormous stage show included dazzling costumes and choreography. She also appeared in highly rated television specials.

Her acting credits were equally impressive. In her first two films she co-starred in one feature with Sidney Poitier and another with Billy Dee Williams. She received an Academy Award nomination for Best Actress for her performance as a slave in a Civil War epic entitled *Plantation*.

However in 1976, things took a downturn. Her long-time love affair with Malcolm Brown became public and erupted into a full-scale scandal. Brown's wife began embarrassing and expensive divorce proceedings costing Brown a good amount of his wealth to achieve a settlement. All this sudden and negative publicity sent Evie on some heavy drinking binges. She was fired from her latest film project and deemed "difficult to work with" in the Hollywood press.

The situation came to a head at a concert on a sultry June night in Atlanta, Georgia. Evie arrived late to the hall and began drinking. She continued to do so throughout her make-up and hair session. Evie went on stage some thirty minutes late and the audience reception was somewhat cold. Her professionalism and showmanship carried her through most of the first half of the show but by the time the "Feel the Love" number came around, she was quite rocky.

Her dance moves were unsteady causing one of her male dancers to stumble and nearly fall throwing her timing off completely. Evie stood center stage with her hand on her hip. She motioned for the orchestra to stop playing.

"No, no, no…just a second, just a second." When things grew quiet she continued, "I'm sorry ladies and gentleman, I apologize – I truly do. I love this song. It's always meant so much to me because it reflects the love I share with my audience. But, to be honest with you kind folks, I *don't* feel the love tonight. I don't feel the love at all. Where is the love, people? Where is the love?"

The stunned audience buzzed. Some boos rang out.

"Shut up and sing girl," an angry male voice called out.

Evie's meltdown continued, "I can recall another evening many years ago when I first came to your fair city with my group the Pixies. No limousine to transport me to the theater back then, no sir. We came in on an old bus. I wasn't allowed to get off the bus and have dinner with the white artists because of the color of my skin. There was no love then either…"

As she rambled on, the audience became unruly. The musical director cued the orchestra and the musicians played loudly to drown out whatever else Evie had to say. The stage went dark. One of her male assistants hurried out and physically removed her from the stage as the curtains closed.

Minutes later, a nervous voice came over the public address system. "We're sorry ladies and gentleman, but due to illness Ms. Rhodes will not be able to complete her performance tonight. Please proceed to the box office for a complete refund on the cost of your tickets. Thank you."

♪ ♪ ♪ ♪ ♪

Great strides occurred in the treatment of drug and

alcohol abuse. Government funding led to the opening of rehab clinics all across the country. Long Beach Naval Hospital in California was one of the more upscale facilities. Perhaps their most famous celebrity client was the former First Lady Betty Ford. Not long after she left the White House, she announced that she had a drinking problem and dependence on opioid analgesics serious enough to warrant treatment.

Another famous, though much-less publicized patient was Evie Rhodes.

Bobby Vitale walked slowly through the wide doors leading to the aviary of the hospital. The duty nurse said he would find Evie there. He carried a bouquet of a dozen roses. Evie sat in a wicker chair dressed in a long housecoat. She appeared gaunt and drawn. Her hair was combed but not styled. She wore no make-up.

When she saw him approach, she let out a hearty laugh. "Well, look who it is. C'mon over here you big good-looking hunk o' man you."

She tried to stand and Bobby hurried over to take her in his arms. He gave her a big smile and a huge hug. "How are you Evie?"

"Oh Bobby, it's so good to see you." With Bobby's help she settled back into her chair.

"I brought you these," he said handing her the flowers.

She took them and breathed deeply to savor the aroma. "They're just beautiful." Bobby pulled up a chair and sat across from her. "Oh Millie?" Evie called out and a young hospital attendant came over. "Will you put these in water and then bring them to my room, please?"

"Certainly Miss Rhodes," the attendant answered taking the flowers and walking away.

"You know, you could have called ahead and given a girl a chance to glamour up a bit. I look like a washed out dish rag."

"That's okay Evie. You've been through a lot."

"I suppose, but I'm getting better."

"I'm glad to hear that."

"So, what brings you out this way?"

"Can't I just drop by and visit an old friend?"

Evie doubted his reason. "You waited all these years until I was in a place like this to catch up?"

"I caught your show a couple of times when you came to Vegas," he said.

"And you didn't come backstage to see me? I'm crushed."

"Couldn't get by your entourage sweetheart. Anyway it's a two-way street. I was playing out there too you know."

"I know. I've been somewhat bitchy these last few years."

"You've always been bitchy," Bobby said with a smile.

Evie let out a laugh. "You can say that to me after all we meant to each other?" They had been secret lovers in the old days. "Remember that first tour we did together? That train ride to DC? Me and you gettin all touchy feely in that Pullman car?"

"We *were* rascally," Bobby agreed.

"Yes we were. But seriously, what's up with you?"

"Well, I'm heading back to New York, for good. I was there a few months ago. We recorded an LP with a couple of covers and updated versions of our hits. It's selling pretty good, especially at concerts. Joe Rabin's reunion shows have really caught on. He's got a whole slew of them scheduled back east, all the way from Massachusetts down to South Florida."

"That's wonderful news Bobby." Evie perked up and moved forward in her chair. "I wrote to Joseph. I told him that Malcolm Brown has made it quite clear that after I get out of this rehab he plans to cut me loose, let me out of my contract. I was hoping maybe Joseph would consider taking me back."

"Joe's not in your league anymore Evie."

"That don't matter," she insisted. "I don't need to have my sights set so high anymore. Heck I'd even hook up with Althea and Roberta again, a Pixies reunion. Now wouldn't that be something?"

A serious look crossed Bobby's face. He had to choose his next words carefully. Evie was in a fragile state. His news could bring about a setback. "I know about the letter you sent Joseph. That's another reason why I came today. He asked me to tell you that he was sorry, but he doesn't have the resources to offer you anything right now."

Evie's eyes went wide and she leaned back. She looked away for a second before gathering herself. "So you're Joseph's messenger boy these days as well?"

"It's not like that at all Evie." Bobby and Joseph had locked horns many times over the years. Not the least of which included the time Bobby caught him and Evie coming out of a midtown hotel together. "Look, Malcolm Brown and Joe Rabin aren't the only two producers in the phone book. Once you've completed this rehab and you're back on your feet, people are going to be calling you with big time offers."

He sounded sincere.

"You've got that right. Listen Bobby, I'm feeling a bit tired. It doesn't help me if I overdue things. Would you mind?"

"Not at all. I understand perfectly." Bobby rose to his feet and leaned in to kiss Evie on her cheek. The warmth he met with on his arrival was gone. "It was good to see you sweetheart. Be well."

"Same here darling. You say hi from me to everyone back east," she managed a smile.

"I will."

He swallowed hard as he turned to go. It had been an unpleasant task to be sure. He'd pleaded with Joseph not to leave it to him to do it. Yet Evie needed to be dealt with. The triangle from the past needed to be broken forever. Now it was done.

Chapter Twenty-One:
"The Beacon"

"Do you have the money?" Jacki Silvestri asked Danielle. The two girls met in front of the lockers on the main floor corridor of Rye High School.

Danielle nodded and answered curtly, "Of course I do. I told you the money was no problem." She worked the combination lock, opened her locker and retrieved an envelope which she handed to Jacki. "There's enough there for three of the highest priced tickets. But you need to get them soon before they're sold out."

"I know…I know," she snatched the envelope from the freshman's hands. "Brian is going downtown right after sixth period. He knows what to do."

"Brian? Brian Devlin? *He's* going with us?"

"Why not? He's a fullback on the football team. You wanted a big guy for protection didn't you? And besides, he likes me…do just about anything I ask him to." She smirked in her conceit.

Danielle simply shook her head.

Jacki was a junior, a tall girl with long brown hair and a good figure. When she made-up and dressed nicely she could easily pass for eighteen. Her mother was a single mom who worked two jobs and didn't have a lot of time to oversee her daughter's social life. That made her a perfect choice to help with Danielle's plan. That and the fact their mothers had never met, meant the two girls could concoct elaborate deceptions and claim that the other's mom gave their approval for a late night of studying or a shopping trip.

Such was the case for this particular scheme. In three weeks, the band Amadeus had a concert scheduled at the Beacon Theater in Manhattan. Danielle wanted to be there but didn't want her parents to know. She agreed to pay for all three tickets with money she squirreled away from her allowance or clothes shopping expenses. Danielle also instructed Jacki to enlist the aid of an older boy, preferably a member of one of the sports teams, to act as chaperone. Each girl then lied to their mother telling them that the other mom was taking them both to the show.

Like most of the band's loyal fans, the main attraction for Danielle was lead singer TJ Russell. Because she liked his music she was willing to put aside the pre-conceived opinion she had of him as a troublemaker and a person at odds with her father. She agreed with what Joseph had to say when she showed him that she bought their first LP.

"Most singers have a voice. This TJ Russell has a sound."

"So then you aren't mad that I like them?" she asked. "Because of what he says about Teddy?"

"No, not at all sweetheart. He's the one holding the grudge, not me."

"I don't think my mom would agree with you."

"Maybe not. But I don't think she's going to throw your album into the fireplace."

Danielle wasn't too sure about that either.

After the band's first single peaked at number three, others reached the top ten with two of those going to number two. They appeared on television shows like Don Kirshner's *Rock Concert*, and of course, *The Midnight Special*. The camera loved Russell, concentrating on his face with a perpetual smile, which seemed to indicate he loved every second he spent on stage. Two albums later they were still at the top of their game and several more top five singles followed.

When the show at the Beacon was announced, Danielle knew she had to be there. It was a simple plan. The New York Central Railroad would take them to Grand Central Station. From there it would only be a short subway ride to 72nd Street, two blocks from the theater.

The other part of the plan, the one Jacki and Brian

wouldn't know anything about might be tricky, but Danielle felt certain she could pull it off.

♪ ♪ ♪ ♪ ♪

Danielle had to admit, Brian did a fine job in getting them great seats in the fifth row center. The opening act was a trio of two males and one female singer performing on acoustic instruments for about thirty minutes. The crowd gave them a warm response.

When Amadeus took the stage, the place went wild. Many in the audience leapt to their feet, screamed and shouted through the band's entire ninety-minute set. The sound was deafening. This was so different from the shows she'd been to that her dad put on. The crowd was younger, charged with electricity and excitement. The pounding beat of the music blasting through the wall of speakers, erected on either side of the stage, bombarded the audience sending a penetrating vibration of sound against their bodies.

Danielle's eyes were riveted on TJ. The way he moved, the way he sang, captivated her. Sometimes on their up-tempo tunes, the audience would engage in a sing-a-long. TJ would come out from behind his microphone exhorting fans by putting his hand up to his ear and shaking his head indicating that he couldn't hear them so they'd sing louder.

After two long thundering encores, the band members stood in a line center stage to take their final bow. A moment later the house lights came up.

"C'mon, come with me," Danielle said as she grabbed Jacki's arm and dragged her toward the end of the aisle.

"Why," Jacki protested. "Where do you think you're going?"

"Just follow my lead okay."

Jacki turned and reached out for Brian. "C'mon."

Brian was confused "Where the..." He was finally pulled along behind.

Danielle's backstage experience gave her insight into the general layout for most concert halls. Still it was no easy task moving against the wave of humanity headed in the opposite direction. She was also aware that sooner or later, a security guard or someone else in authority would challenge their progress before they reached their destination.

They were stopped at a curtained off area by a rather large black member of the security staff. "You can't go back there Miss."

"I know I'm not supposed to," Danielle said in a feigned shaky voice. "Is there anybody back there from the record company?" She knew there would be. "Myriad Records? There should be somebody back there."

"Yeah, I think so," the man replied.

"Could you please, would you please bring him out here? It's very important that I speak to him, really very important." Danielle sounded quite convincing.

"Alright. You wait right here though." He turned to one of his colleagues. "Make sure these kids stay right here."

The guard moved through the curtain. Jacki spun Danielle around to face her. "You're trying to get us backstage? Are you crazy?"

"Shhh…be quiet…this is gonna work." She kept her head facing away from the security guard and pinched her cheeks.

"What the heck are you doing?"

"Trying to make myself cry."

Before Jacki could ask another question, the security guard returned. He had another younger man with him. This man had long hair, glasses and was dressed in a plaid shirt and jeans.

"This is Mr. Calhoun. He's with the record company," the guard said.

"What can I do for you sweetheart?" Calhoun asked.

Danielle's deception worked. She had genuine tears in her eyes when she spoke. "Oh, Mr. Calhoun, thank God. My name is Ellie Franklin, I'm Artie Franklin's grand niece."

The sound of his boss's name caused him to give this girl his complete attention. "I didn't know Artie Franklin had a ..."

Danielle cut him off, "That doesn't matter. You see, he sent me three tickets and back stage passes as a birthday present. I lost the back stage passes and if my father finds out he's gonna kill me. I just have to get back there and meet the band or else I'm in real trouble." Her story was full of holes and she knew it, but everything around them was happening so fast. She depended on the confusion to help her succeed.

"Listen kid, I can't let you back there. I don't know nothing about this."

"Well, I could suggest that you call my grand uncle in Memphis, but then I'd really get in trouble and you'd probably lose your job." She was no longer crying.

"Alright, alright, alright. I'll bring you back for five minutes. Got that? Five minutes. Follow me."

Calhoun led the way with the three teenagers hurrying behind. The corridors in the back area were alive with activity. Roadies and members of the breakdown crew worked feverishly. Press, radio people and legitimate VIP's stood in line in front of the door to a reception room. Calhoun went to the head of the line and opened the door, holding it to allow Danielle and her two friends to enter over the protests of many.

"Hey, where are they going?"

"What the fuck?"

"What's this cutting the line bullshit? We were here first."

"Everybody just calm down," Calhoun shot back. "You'll all get your chance."

Inside the spacious room, tables and chairs were set up. Along one wall, a large buffet table stood loaded with food. Ice buckets chilling champagne bottles were everywhere promising a wonderful celebration. However, it wasn't a celebration taking place in the far corner of the room where Danielle and the others could easily see and hear the members of Amadeus engaged in a heated argument.

TJ Russell was in the face of the band's drummer.

"You messed up the cue in that last encore number and I damn near missed my mark. What the fuck is wrong with you man?"

"I'm sorry man. The crowd was so loud tonight. I couldn't hear a goddam thing."

"We've played that song the exact same way for the last thirty straight gigs. You shouldn't have to hear it. You should be able to feel it by now."

"We can't all be geniuses like you man," Cam Pierson added sarcastically.

TJ turned his attention Pierson's way. "Well, that's too bad isn't it? You know, if I could, I'd go out there and play all the fucking instruments myself."

"Why don't you try that sometime genius?"

"Maybe I will – sometime."

What seemed like such a happy, cohesive unit just minutes ago onstage had turned into something more akin to a bunch of bickering schoolboys arguing on a playground. TJ showed himself to be an arrogant conceited bully.

Calhoun's voice broke up the argument. "Hey, guys...guys...simmer down we got company." As he ushered the group forward, TJ's attitude changed drastically. He approached them like a true superstar. In true lecherous fashion, he put his arm around Jacki and kissed her squarely on the lips. "What's *your* name sweetheart?"

Jacki was stunned into silence.

Calhoun broke up the embrace. "Fellas, I'd like you meet Ellie Franklin, she's Artie's grand niece."

"Grand niece? The old fart has a family?" Russell blurted out.

Danielle was shocked by the singer's behavior. "You're nothing but an obnoxious asshole. You know that?"

"What?" TJ lashed out. "Who do you think you're talking to? I don't care who you are…you can forget about getting any kind of autograph."

"I don't want *anything* from you. You claim to be Teddy Boyette's son? You couldn't shine Teddy's shoes."

Russell fumed and fought to control his temper. "Did anyone ever tell you you're a real snot nosed kid? Get these runts outta here."

"C'mon you kids," Calhoun shooed the three of them out of the room.

🎵🎵🎵🎵🎵

They caught a late train out of Penn Station and sat in a car that was nearly empty. Emboldened by the excitement of the evening, Brian had his arm around Jacki. Danielle sat across the aisle from them.

"I can't believe TJ Russell kissed me," Jackie said as though in a trance.

"Yeah, well, you better take a hot shower when you get home. I wouldn't be surprised if he has cooties," Danielle warned.

"I don't care if he does have cooties."

Brian finally spoke up. "And I can't believe that Dani told him off like that. I thought you liked the guy?"

"I did too," she replied, "but when I saw him tearing into that other guy, I saw him for what he really was…a jerk."

"You called him an asshole," Brian reminded her.

Danielle giggled, "Yeah, I know."

"And who is this Teddy Boyette?" Brian asked.

Jacki knew the answer. "A famous singer from the old days. He was a friend of Dani's mom and dad."

"Wow," Brian was impressed.

Chapter Twenty-Two:
"Demolition and Radiation"

Musical trends were changing once again. Disco music was on the decline and the public became outspoken in their dislike for the genre. Long-haired hippie types walked around with T-shirts emblazoned with "Disco Sucks" across the front.

In Chicago, a popular morning radio disc jockey, Steve Dahl created an all out campaign against disco music. He convinced Mike Veeck, the promotions head of Major League Baseball's Chicago White Sox franchise to stage a *Disco Demolition Night*. The event was to take place between games of a double-header between the White Sox and the Detroit Tigers. If a fan turned in a disco record at the gate they could attend the game for just 98 cents.

By mid-July, the team was playing under five hundred ball and languished in the bottom half of the American League's Western Division. Attendance figures fell to less than six thousand fans per game. Mike's father Bill Veeck, the team's owner, had often given his okay to many outlandish type promotions.

On the Demolition Night, Thursday July 12, over 70,000 fans arrived at Comiskey Park carrying disco 45's or LPs. After a time, ticket takers stopped collecting the records. Fans soon found a better use for them and tossed them onto the field like Frisbees. The game was delayed as groundskeepers cleared the field of play.

By the second inning, the smell of marijuana permeated the ballpark. The White Sox lost the first game 4-1.

Between games, stadium staff rolled a huge box containing the records out to center field. Dahl appeared wearing army fatigues and a helmet. He conducted a countdown and then detonated explosives rigged into the box. Shards of vinyl, and pieces of the container went flying. A billow of smoke rose from a small fire which started in the outfield grass. The crowd erupted into an immense frenzy.

After removing the box and extinguishing the fire, preparations were made to begin the second game. Fans began to wander out onto the diamond. Hundreds more followed before the White Sox players relinquished the field to them. A fan shimmied his way down the foul pole from the upper deck in right field. Someone started a bonfire, bases were stolen and home plate was dug completely out of the ground.

Police in riot gear arrived to clear the crowd. Even with longtime White Sox broadcaster Harry Carey cajoling them to join in and sing "Take Me Out to the Ballgame," nothing could be done. Umpires ruled the field unplayable and called off the second game. The next day, the Commissioner of Baseball announced that the White Sox would forfeit the game to Detroit.

By the end of September, there was not a single disco record anywhere in the top ten.

♪ ♪ ♪ ♪ ♪

Musicians United for Safe Energy, sometimes known as MUSE, was an activist group created by Jackson Browne, Graham Nash, John Hall and Bonnie Raitt to speak out against the use of nuclear energy. The group formed shortly after the Three Mile Island nuclear accident.

On March 28, 1979, at the Three Mile Island power plant in Pennsylvania, a pilot-operated relief valve became stuck in the open position. Plant operators were slow to identify the problem and correct it. As a result, large amounts of radioactive gasses and iodine were released into the atmosphere. In addition, 40,000 gallons of radioactive waste water was released directly into the Susquehanna River. It was the worst incident in US Power Plant history.

MUSE organized a series of star-studded concerts to be held at New York's Madison Square Garden. A rally attended by over 200,000 people was staged at the Battery Park landfill.

The finale of the shows was an exhilarating performance of Gary US Bond's song "A Quarter to Three" done by a hugely popular artist of the day, Bruce Springsteen and the E-Street Band.

Chapter Twenty-Three:
"The Holy Land"

In the fall, Janet accepted an offer from her New York Publisher to travel to Israel to photograph the Holy Land for a new coffee table book. The project excited her.

"It's really a once in a lifetime opportunity," she said over dinner at home. "I'd like to take Dani with me."

On hearing this, their daughter beamed, "Oh can I Daddy?"

"What about school?" Joseph asked.

"I can speak to her teachers. They can prepare work for her to do while we're away."

"It's a dangerous part of the world. There's a revolution going on somewhere, isn't there?"

"Yes, in Iran, but that's a thousand miles away," Janet replied.

Not so very far for a missile, Joseph thought to himself.

"Think of all the neat stories I'll have to tell grandma Myra when I visit her in Florida," Danielle offered.

"If you're going to bring your grandmother into this conversation to help convince me, I don't see where I have much choice. You'll need a passport."

Danielle became all giddy and rushed to hug him. "Oh, thank you Daddy." She took a breath before turning to Janet. "And clothes, lots and lots of new clothes, right Mom?"

Janet laughed loudly. "Yes, I suppose so for both of us."

"*Oy-vey,*" Joseph responded before laughing himself.

♫♫♫♫♫

Since the end of World War II, hundreds of thousands of displaced European Jews flocked to the Middle East to an area known as British Mandate Palestine. The Jewish people considered this area the Promised Land dating back to the biblical times of King David.

On May 15, 1948, the United Nations declared the establishment of the State of Israel. The very next day, the tiny nation, roughly the size of New Jersey, withstood an invasion by five of its Arab neighbors. One year later, a ceasefire ended the war and temporary borders were established. Since then, hostilities ranging from all-out war to terrorist attacks against both military and civilian targets became commonplace.

In 1978, Egyptian President Anwar el-Sadat, Israeli Prime Minister Menachem Begin and US President Jimmy Carter, met at Camp David in Maryland to hammer out a peace treaty. With the signing of the Camp David Accord, Egypt became the first Arab nation to recognize Israel.

♪♪♪♪♪

Janet and Danielle arrived in Tel-Aviv, Israel late in October. The publishing company put them up in a luxury hotel with a magnificent view of the Mediterranean Sea. After a good night's sleep from their long flights, they ate a hearty breakfast and were introduced to their interpreter and driver by the hotel manager.

The driver of their leased Volkswagen Van was an older man named Avram who spoke no English. Their translator was a pretty Israeli girl, Shira Bar-On. No older than eighteen, she stood five feet five with light complexion and almond-brown eyes conveying a wisdom beyond her years. Her long black hair was pulled in a bun at the back of her head. She wore a short sleeve kaki button down shirt with matching shorts, green socks and army boots. Her English betrayed the slight hint of an accent.

"Shira, this is Mrs. Rabinowitz and her daughter Danielle," the manager said.

"Pleased to meet you both." She reached out to shake Janet's hand then bowed her head to Danielle who nodded back.

"That's a cute outfit," Danielle said.

Shira smiled. "It was part of my IDF uniform."

"IDF?"

"Israeli Defense Force."

"Defense force? You were in the army? But, you're so young."

The hotel manager spoke up, "In Israel we expect our young people to mature very quickly Miss."

"You wish to go to the Holy City today?" Shira asked Janet changing the subject.

"Jerusalem, yes," Janet confirmed.

"There is much to see there. We should be on our way."

"Certainly. We're all set."

♫♫♫♫♫

Jerusalem was considered the holiest of cities for the world's three major religions, Christianity, Judaism and Islam. The city had been destroyed twice, captured and recaptured over forty times and was now politically and militarily under the control of Israel.

Within the walls of the Old City, several of the world's holiest places were located. Janet's assignment was to photograph them all. She began in the Muslim sector, at the Dome of the Rock, an Islamic shrine located on the Temple Mount. They continued to the nearby al-Aqsa Mosque known as the place where the Prophet Muhammad began his journey to Heaven.

For Christians, the Church of the Holy Sepulcher marked the area where Jesus Christ was crucified and rose from the dead. Jews revered the site of the Temple Mount as the place where God dwells. The Babylonians destroyed the first Temple built by King Solomon in biblical times. Romans destroyed the second Temple after banning all Jews from the Roman Empire. A 187-foot section of the Temple's western wall remained and became a sacred place for Jewish prayer commonly referred to as The Wailing Wall.

♪♪♪♪♪

Danielle watched as her mother worked with an intensity and diligence she'd never seen before. Each photo she took had to be from exactly the right angle, display the right amount of light and shadow. The images in her viewfinder had to portray the natural reverence of these holy places.

Even when they stopped for lunch, Janet sometimes rose from her chair to get a spontaneous shot of something or someone of interest.

"Your mother truly loves her work," Shira remarked.

"Yeah," Danielle answered. "All this time I thought she just took pictures."

"Perhaps she feels the solemnity of her surroundings?"

"I don't know what you mean."

"Being here, being Jewish. Your family name 'Rabinowitz.' You *are* Jewish, yes?"

"My dad is Jewish, my step dad that is," Danielle explained. "My mom was brought up Catholic. My real father was from England. I can't recall him being religious of any kind. I guess you could say, beyond some holiday observances, none of us really practice at anything."

"I imagine you do things very differently in America," Shira commented.

"*Ab-so-tute-ly.*"

"Pardon?"

Danielle laughed. "Oh, that's just some word bending game we play back home. It's silly I know."

"Silly, yes, but it sounds like fun Danielle."

"Yes, it *is* fun. We do it with names too, so from now on, I want you to call me Dani, okay?"

"All right…Dani."

Just then, two Arab boys stopped at their table pushing

trinkets in front their faces. Shira shooed them away with a stern look and scolding Arabic phrases.

"Just how many languages do you speak anyway?"

"Hebrew, Yiddish and English certainly…Arabic and most Aramaic dialects."

"Wow. I can hardly get by in my Spanish class at school."

"Oh Dani, you make me laugh so."

"Why? What did I do?"

"The way you say things. *Wow* is such a little word but when you say it, it seems to carry such importance. I should like to visit America one day."

"Sure. It's a great place. You should get your parents to take you."

Shira became solemn. "I'm an orphan. My parents were killed in a rocket attack in nineteen-seventy-one."

"Oh my God Shira, I'm so sorry. A rocket attack?"

"Yes, I'm afraid it is a danger we here in Israel have come to learn to live with."

"Well, I don't think *I* could *ever* learn to live with something like that."

"That's why you Americans are so very lucky." Shira wanted to change the subject. "If I ever came to America, where should I visit?"

"Oh, without a doubt, New York City. If, for no other reason, than the great food. Great Chinese, pizza, dirty water hot dogs."

Shira interrupted her. "I know what a hot dog is…but do they *really* make it in dirty water?"

"Well, no…I mean yes…I mean… that really doesn't matter as long as you have it with mustard and onions and sauerkraut."

The two girls laughed heartily.

♫ ♫ ♫ ♫ ♫

Over the next few days, their party visited more places. They toured the cities near the Sea of Galilee, in reality a freshwater lake of the Jordan River, to see the place where Jesus Christ gave the Sermon on the Mount.

On the road back to Tel-Aviv from a photo shoot at King David's Tomb on Mount Zion, they stopped at a small marketplace on the road. While Janet shopped for a shawl, Danielle and Shira wandered off across the plaza to look at tables containing jewelry and other knickknacks.

"What are those?" Danielle asked Shira.

"Those are Mezuzahs. Jewish people hang them outside their doorways as a blessing to all who enter. Each one of these cases contains a piece of parchment with verses from the Torah. All Jews should display one."

Danielle picked one up to take a closer look. "Oooo this one is real pretty. How much is it?"

Shira spoke Hebrew to the man behind the table. The longer they talked the louder and more animated the conversation became.

"What's wrong?" Danielle asked.

"He claims the case is pure silver. He's asking much too much for it."

"Oh Shira, it's so beautiful. Please see what you can do."

As Shira continued to bargain with the man, Danielle noticed her mother looking at a table not far from where they were. She hurried over certain that if she explained the situation to her, she would surely intercede.

On their way back to the jewelry table Shira met them. She didn't look happy.

"I'm sorry Dani, he wouldn't budge on the price."

"Ohhh," Danielle said with great disappointment.

"Don't worry," Shira consoled her. "We'll find something just like it someplace else."

Recognizing that all work and no play was not much

fun at all, Janet declared a two-day hiatus from work. They spent the time relaxing on a Mediterranean beach. Shira agreed to join them. On the second night, Janet treated them to dinner at an elegant restaurant in Tel-Aviv. There, Janet laid out the plan for their next excursion.

"I'd like to go and tour Masada tomorrow," she told Shira.

"A very wonderful trip. But rather a hardship," their translator explained, "the path leading up to the plateau is very winding and difficult."

On hearing this, Danielle griped. "I don't know about that Mom."

Shira had a plan. "If I may, I can have Avram carry your equipment up the path while Danielle and I wait for you below. I'm reasonably sure you can make yourself understood to him."

"Yes I'm sure I can as well. All right, we'll get an early start."

The drive to Masada proved one of stark contrasts. At some points along the road, one side opened up to vast arid desert landscapes, while the other featured fields of lush greenery. Avram paid attention to the road and the two teenagers chattered away, Janet envisioned caravans of nomads roaming the desert on majestic camels. She imagined shepherds tending great flocks of sheep in the fields.

Masada proved to be an emotional and heart wrenching experience. The mountain fortress was the site where nearly one thousand Jews were besieged by a Roman Legion. When the Romans finally reached the summit they found all the defenders had committed mass suicide rather than submit themselves to slavery. Janet feared her pictures could never capture the sense of solemnity of the locale.

Days later, Janet and Danielle came out of their hotel and were greeted by a bustle of activity and wailing sirens.

Several jeeps and trucks whizzed through the streets loaded with armed soldiers.

"Shira has something happened here?" Janet asked with concern.

"No ma'am…not here…in Iran. Some militant students have stormed the US Embassy there and taken many hostages."

"But my father said Iran was like a thousand miles away. Why all this here?" asked Danielle.

"It's just a precaution. Our military has been put on alert. It is feared that if your President Carter retaliates, we may suffer some reprisals here."

Danielle shook her head. "That's just nuts."

"It's…"

Danielle cut her off, "Yeah, I know. It's just something people here in Israel have learned to live with."

Chapter Twenty-Four:
"Iran"

In 1953 the nation of Iran, formerly known as Persia, saw its democratic government ousted in a Coup D'état financed by the Central Intelligence Agency of the United States and supported by the military forces of Great Britain. The Iranian government nationalized the British owned oil industry leading to an embargo by the west and the eventual coup that returned the Shah, Mohammad Reza Pahlavi, to the throne.

Over the years the Shah took steps to *westernize* his country, a plan many criticized as a "White Revolution." This met with great opposition by religious leaders, including an Islamic cleric, Ayatollah Ruhollah Khomeni. He characterized America as "The Great Satan" and called for the overthrow of the Shah's regime. Fearing the Ayatollah's growing popularity, the Shah exiled him to France.

An Islamic Revolution took place in Iran with demonstrations crippling the nation. The Shah was eventually forced to flee the country and Khomeni returned from exile. Iran's military declared itself neutral while rebel troops overthrew the Pahlavi Dynasty. Iran became an Islamic Republic in 1979.

On November 4, 1979, a mob of over 300 militant students stormed the US Embassy in Tehran chanting that the building housed a "den of spies." They took over 60 military and civilian men and women hostage. The students paraded the handcuffed and blindfolded hostages through the streets for the entire world to see.

US President Jimmy Carter urged restraint in reacting to this crisis and vowed that the United States would never give in to the demands of terrorists. He began an intense campaign to resolve the situation through diplomatic channels. The president then seized more than eight billion dollars in financial assets. The measures had no effect whatsoever. The stalemate began.

♫ ♫ ♫ ♫ ♫

"I'm so sorry you have to cut your trip short," Shira told Janet. They waited curbside at Tel-Aviv Airport. Avram unloaded the luggage and camera equipment from the van. Danielle leaned against the front of the vehicle. She was sad.

"I am too," Janet explained, "but my husband is worried for our safety."

"I understand."

"I want you to have this," Janet held out a white envelope and handed it to the young girl, "to show our appreciation for everything you've done."

"That's not necessary," she protested.

"Oh, nonsense. Of course it is. I have something for Avram as well. Say your farewells to Dani while I give it to him."

As Janet headed off to find their driver, Shira walked up to Danielle.

"I'm going to miss you Dani," Shira told her.

"It's not fair. The stupid war is thousands of miles away."

"Your father is worried for you."

"I know. But if Israelis can go about life as though nothing was going on, why can't we?"

"You should be happy that you live in place where you don't have to worry about such things." Shira handed her a small item wrapped in a piece of cloth. "I have something for you."

"What is it?" Danielle wiped a tear from her cheek.

"See for yourself."

Danielle rolled out the cloth to reveal the Mezuzah she admired while shopping just days before. The sight of it brought a smile to her face.

"But I thought you said…"

"I knew it wasn't solid silver," she confessed with a smile of her own. "I just didn't want you to buy it yourself."

They embraced warmly and kissed one another on both cheeks.

"You have my address," Danielle reminded her, "and you *will* write to me, right?"

"*Ab-so-tute-ly*," Shira said with a huge smile.

They embraced again one last time.

Chapter Twenty-Five:
"John's Bargain Store Cheap"

The death knell for disco music rang out on the evening of February 27th, 1980. The 22nd Annual Grammy Awards presented at the Shrine Auditorium in Los Angeles, California, featured a new category for Best Disco Performance. The nominees included Earth, Wind and Fire for "Boogie Wonderland," Michael Jackson for "Don't Stop Till You Get Enough," Gloria Gaynor for "I Will Survive," Rod Stewart for "Do Ya Think I'm Sexy?" and Donna Summer for "Bad Girls."

It came as no surprise when "I Will Survive" won the award.

Since its release, the tune became a worldwide smash. It went to number one on the *Billboard* Hot 100 Chart and remained there for three weeks. Written and produced by Dino Fekaris and Freddie Perren, the song displayed the defiance and determination of a woman in the throes of a terrible emotional upheaval and her ability to pick herself up, brush herself off and survive whatever life threw her way. When the spoken-word intro played through the speakers of discos around the world, women flocked to the dance floor in droves.

Despite the recognition this disco anthem received, the National Academy of Recording Arts and Sciences dropped the Best Disco Recording category the very next year.

♫ ♫ ♫ ♫ ♫

When their first three-year contract with Myriad Records ran out, the group Amadeus signed a second and more lucrative four-year deal taking them into 1981. By the spring of 1980, they became the top LP act in the business. They placed five consecutive singles as high as number two on the charts, yet the number one spot eluded them. Whether it was some trashy disco tune or a solid effort by chart perennials like Paul McCartney, John Lennon, Queen or the new wave group Blondie, Amadeus became the clichéd bridesmaid and never the bride.

This didn't hold well with TJ Russell at all. The terms of the new contract now stipulated that he and Cam Pierson share songwriting credits, a detail that irked Pierson. Meanwhile, TJ came to think of the others as an anvil around his neck, keeping him from an achievement he considered his birthright. He was determined to reach the crowning moment of his career and didn't want to wait years to do it.

So it was that he found himself incognito in New York City headed to an appointment with Richie Conforti, the top executive at Alexis Records.

♪♪♪♪♪

Nearing eighty, Max Seiderman still possessed a sharp mind for financial matters. Though his well-qualified staff now handled the day to day accounting business for the Viola crime syndicate, Seiderman maintained the go-between role with Richie Conforti and the head of the family.

The former Don, Gugliemo Viola died in 1978. His oldest son Carlo became the new Don. Under his guidance, the family moved into the highly lucrative area of gun running. He had little patience for minor operations like Alexis Records. But he knew Max since childhood, so when the older man requested a sit down, Carlo agreed to see him. The two men sat at a table on the apron of the patio on the Long Island estate.

Carlo was giving Max a hard time.

"The record company was like a hobby for the old man, like a fucking stamp collection or something. It's been siphoning money for years. Why should I put more into it now?"

"Your father *never* expected the place to make money.

He saw it as an investment, a write-off at tax time. But Conforti and Gambetta surprised everybody and brought in a ton of cash for a good long time. This Russell kid they wanna sign is no washed up oldies act. He's current. You give him the contract he wants and he's gonna pay big dividends right off. I'm telling you Carlo, this is a good move."

Carlo asked, "And what about the other thing, the black bitch?"

"Evie Rhodes? That's different."

"She's nothing but fucking trouble. Everybody says so."

"She still has value though. She's a perfect pigeon…an addict. We can take advantage of that. All she needs is a babysitter. I got the perfect guy in mind, a former linebacker with the Jets. He'll service her, keep her happy and make sure she stays in line. Besides, we can sign her cheap."

"How cheap?"

"John's Bargain Store cheap." Max made reference to a successful chain of retail discount stores popular in the sixties. Carlo understood perfectly.

"You're a smart Jew, Max, always have been. And the old man thought of you as a friend. So because of that, I'm gonna okay the money. But those dividends better come soon like you said."

♫ ♫ ♫ ♫ ♫

When news got around regarding TJ's defection from Amadeus, the reaction was almost immediate.

Cam Pierson called Russell a traitor. His expletive-laden quote was heavily bleeped when televised. "Fuck him. He's an ungrateful bastard in the true sense of the word. He doesn't know how to be part of a team. We're better off without the selfish prick."

Record company executive Artie Franklin remained calm over the situation, but announced that he would sue TJ

Russell for breach of contract.

Two nights later, a three-alarm fire destroyed a warehouse and distribution center for not only Myriad Records, but Stax Records and several other major Memphis recording companies. The estimated cost of losses was in the hundreds of thousands of dollars. An investigation determined that arson was the cause of the blaze.

Without further fanfare, Artie Franklin dropped his lawsuit.

Chapter Twenty-Six:
"Operation Eagle Claw"

"It's been five months and nobody has done anything about it at all." Danielle complained as she and her parents sat watching the evening news. She referred to the continuing hostage crises in Iran.

By this time, most of the networks featured a small graphic at the bottom of their broadcast feed indicating the number of days the hostages remained prisoners. The number read: "169 Days in Captivity."

"President Carter is trying his best to negotiate their release," Janet said.

"His best, really?" Danielle said with sarcasm.

"I even heard that the boxer Muhammad Ali offered to take the hostages place if the Ayatollah agreed," Joseph said.

Danielle had more to say. "In the meantime, people like my friend Shira have to put up with armed soldiers in the streets. Why do they have to live like that? Daddy somebody has to do something soon."

Danielle stood and walked angrily out of the room.

"She's too young to have to deal with this," Joseph said to Janet.

"I was afraid of the bombs once, remember?"

He did recall the time, not long after they first married, Janet was experiencing nightmares. Science fiction movies of the time masked the fear of atomic weapons within their storylines. Green monsters from space replaced the Red Menace from Russia. Recognizing the ploy, she feared the communists would most certainly unleash nuclear war upon the whole world. Joseph, in his loving way assured her that all would be well and quelled her concerns.

"You weren't fifteen."

"I know. It's a different world. But you see what she's done with the yellow ribbons?" The property around the Rabinowitz home contained a number of trees of various sizes and types. Danielle learned that many American citizens tied yellow ribbons around tree trunks where they would remain until the hostages were released. Joseph told her the idea stemmed from a number one song recorded earlier in the decade called "Tie a Yellow Ribbon Round the Old Oak Tree," sung by a group named Dawn. The tune told of a man released from prison who is unsure if his wife and family will welcome him back home. He asks that if she still wants him to tie a yellow ribbon around the oak tree outside their house. When the bus he's riding on turns the corner, he sees all the trees around his home decorated with yellow ribbons.

The practice seemed appropriate once again. "She was the first one to put them up in the area. And she's gone all along Halstead Avenue making sure every house has one. I'm really kinda proud of her."

Joseph smiled. "So am I."

♫♫♫♫♫

In April a newly formed anti-terrorist unit within the military called the Delta Force was commissioned to attempt a rescue of the hostages. The mission was designated: Operation Eagle Claw.

Dispatched from the aircraft carrier USS Nimitz, eight helicopters took part in the mission. Mother Nature intervened in the form of a sandstorm causing one helicopter to crash land and damaged a second so seriously that it had to turn back to the carrier. The remaining airships reached the rendezvous point where a third helicopter damaged its hydraulic system and could not continue. Since a minimum of six aircraft was needed to complete the operation successfully, President Jimmy Carter himself scrubbed the mission.

While refueling for their return flight, one chopper collided with a C-130 tanker aircraft and crashed. Eight US servicemen died and others were wounded.

In a televised report, a somber disgraced American

President described the botched rescue attempt in detail from the Oval Office. It was a devastating moment for the Carter administration, especially in an election year.

Chapter Twenty-Seven:
"The Baby Boomers"

In 1980, an author named Landon Y. Jones, wrote a book called *Great Expectations: America & the Baby Boom Generation*. In the book he coined the term "baby boomers." He described his work as a generational biography, a social analysis of what he called "the most decisive generation in our history. It is above all, the biggest, richest and best educated generation America has ever produced."

The "boom" years was described as the period between 1946 and 1964. During that time 76,441,000 babies were born in America. This averaged out to at least 4 million births in each of those years.

A "baby boom" to be sure.

♫♫♫♫♫

"Watch it, watch it!" Bobby Vitale called out, "I'm hung up on this step here." He was on the lower end of the narrow staircase in the Seracino house. He and Johnny labored to maneuver a queen size mattress down the stairs. Johnny stood at the top of the second floor landing.

Johnny's wife Barbara called for help. "Steven, come in and help these guys before one of them gets hurt."

"Leave the kid alone Barb, we can do this," Johnny said.

Their son Steven, now a handsome young man of twenty-two bounced into the house through the back door and hurried to the stairs. "Okay Uncle Bobby, I'll get that."

Bobby didn't protest when the young man took hold of the mattress and freed it from its obstruction.

"Okay, Dad lets go straight down and out."

The two of them moved quickly now, guiding the mattress down along the main floor and out the back door to where the white van from the Morris Park Lumber Yard waited.

Steven Seracino was getting married in a week's time. He and his fiancée Pamela rented a house not far away on Pelham Parkway. Johnny and Barbara decided to give his old bed to Bobby.

Since his return from Las Vegas a few weeks before, Bobby stayed in Johnny's basement. Recently, he rented a studio apartment above the Lumber Yard that became available for an affordable rent. The bed was a good start in furnishing it. Steven even agreed to let Bobby have the portable television he had in his room. An old dining room set the Liebermanns stored in their garage would be their contribution to Bobby's new digs. They brought it with them for this afternoon barbecue.

Later, the group of family and friends relaxed in the spacious backyard enjoying a warm mid-summer day. Johnny stood at the barbecue grilling hamburgers and hot dogs, along with sweet and hot Italian sausages. The women, in true fashion, were up and around helping. Barbara baked a large tray of eggplant parmesan. Kenny Liebermann's wife Jeannie prepared and served a salad. The younger females, Johnny's twenty-year old daughter Marie and Steven's red-haired fiancée helped set the large table.

After dinner, Steven sat at the red wooden picnic table. Bobby and Kenny Liebermann relaxed on the grass in lawn chairs drinking Bartles and James wine coolers. The oldies station, WCBS-FM, blared through a radio.

"Did you talk to your parents yet?" Marie asked Pamela.

"About what?" Steven answered.

"I wasn't talking to you dweeb. Did she ask her folks about letting Daddy sing at the wedding."

"No I haven't," Pamela answered sheepishly.

"Lay off Marie," Stevie stood up for his girlfriend, "we've got a million things to do before the wedding that are more important than that."

Marie was persistent. "What's the big deal? I don't see how they can say no. Daddy's group was famous and you're his son. You'd think they'd be honored."

"I don't think it'll be a problem," Pamela said in her own defense.

"Hey Stevie," Bobby called out from his chair, "if your future in-laws don't like doo-wop, we can do some Beatles stuff."

Everyone laughed.

When the sun was gone, Johnny lit several tiki shaped citronella lamps around the perimeter of the backyard. The kids left after they finished eating, leaving the adults to enjoy some mellow moments. They talked about the bright future on the horizon for the Du-Kanes.

"So, Joe Rabin tells me the Rye City Council has put him in charge of all the entertainment they're going to be doing at Rye Playland this season. There's gonna be concerts every Friday and Saturday night free to the public. He's guaranteed us one weekend every month," Johnny told the others.

"Free?" Kenny asked. "You mean we don't get paid?"

"We'll get paid by the town," Bobby explained.

There would be other opportunities as well. Joseph was getting a lot of requests from fund raising organizations to promote oldies concerts in schools and other venues. The Du-Kanes and the Pixies would get an ample portion of that work.

Bobby decided to have some innocent fun at Barbara's expense. She was seated at the picnic table with her back to him. He gave Johnny the hi-sign before he spoke, "Ya know Barb, you didn't have to go to all the trouble of hauling Stevie's bed out of his room. I mean, I coulda just moved in here with you guys permanently."

"Yeah right," Barbara giggled. "Honey, I'd adopt you if I didn't have to feed you." Her comeback made everyone laugh.

"No chance of that," Johnny commented. "My wife wants to keep Steven's room empty in case he ever needs to come back."

"Why would he come back?" Jeannie asked.

"In case the marriage don't work," Johnny added.

Barbara became annoyed. "Don't say things like that Johnny. I like Pam. She's gonna make Steven a good wife…and a good mother when the time comes."

"No rush on that," her husband said.

"At least *they* waited." Everyone knew what Barbara meant.

"Maybe they were just better at being careful," said Bobby.

"Oh, shut up you!" Barbara threw a rolled up napkin toward Bobby, but it fell to the ground well short of its mark. "Jeannie, don't you have any single friends we can hook this guy up with so he won't be such a pain in the ass?"

Kenny had a candidate. "How about that one Karen from Edgewater? She just got divorced right?"

Johnny thought he knew her. "Isn't she the one with the big…"

"Hey, hey," Bobby interrupted. "Don't forget I spent a lot of time in Vegas, tits don't impress me. Besides, I don't need to be hooked up with anybody. I'm happy just the way I am."

Barbara knew that even as a teenager Bobby had a love 'em and leave 'em attitude about girls, finding no pleasure in monogamous relationships. An adoring female fan eager to share his bed for a night of passion was all he required from a woman. And besides, he and the divorcee Karen from Edgewater were already well acquainted.

It grew late and the glow from the torches dwindled. Bobby yawned as he stood. "Well, I'm gonna go and enjoy my last night on the couch in your basement. Tomorrow I'll set up my new place and I'll be out of your hair."

He walked to meet Barbara as she stood. "I made you a tray of eggplant so you won't starve…for a week or so anyway," she told him as they embraced.

"You're too good to me Barb."

"I know."

Chapter Twenty-Eight:
"Bedtime For Bonzo"

During his acting career, handsome leading man Ronald Reagan portrayed three larger than life historical figures, George Gipp, a 1920's star football for Notre Dame University, Major League pitching great Grover Cleveland Alexander and George Armstrong Custer, a Civil War General and Indian fighter killed at the Battle of the Little Big Horn.

One of his more dubious roles came in 1951 in a comedy called *Bedtime for Bonzo*. In this movie he played a college professor Peter Boyd, who tries to teach human morals to a chimpanzee by pretending to be the chimp's father.

Beginning in 1947, Reagan held the office of President of the Screen Actors Guild for seven consecutive one-year terms. In that capacity, he testified before the House Committee on Un-American Activities during the McCarthy Hearings to root out communists in the entertainment industry. In televised sessions he never "named names" of any of his colleagues, but he *did* become an informant for the FBI.

In 1954, Reagan signed on to host the CBS-TV dramatic anthology series, *General Electric Theater*. The show became popular and Reagan was hired as spokesman for the company. He toured the country making speeches to the over 250,000 GE employees in forty states. For six years, the Democrat Reagan honed his craft as a speaker. When his speeches began to reflect his own political views rather than Hollywood gossip and selling washing machines, GE warned him to "get back on track." When he refused, they fired him. His liberal views changed radically during the GE years. Adopting a more pro-business, anti-union attitude, he switched affiliations and became a Republican explaining, "I didn't leave the democratic party. The party left me."

Reagan then considered going into politics. He solidified his political agenda in 1964 in a speech supporting the Republican presidential candidate Barry Goldwater. The speech so impressed big money interests in California that they asked him to run for governor. He was elected in 1967 and served two terms. During that time he made two unsuccessful attempts to become the Republican candidate for president in 1968 and 1976.

He decided to try again in 1980.

In Washington, setbacks plagued the Carter administration. The unresolved hostage crisis and botched rescue mission in Iran, the Russian invasion of Afghanistan and our deplorable economic situation at home, were all factors which did not bode well for democrats.

In an outdoor speech in Manhattan, with the Statue of Liberty in the background, Ronald Reagan, dressed in shirtsleeves told a crowd, "A recession is when your best friend loses *his* job. A depression is when *you* lose *your* job. And a recovery is when Jimmy Carter loses *his* job."

In November, Ronald Reagan was elected the 40th President of the United States.

Chapter Twenty-Nine:
"Imagine"

Only uneaten pizza crusts and oil stains remained in the boxes from Enzo's Pizza Shop sitting on the coffee table in the Liebermann living room. Several empty beer bottles were strewn about as well.

The Monday night ritual in Kenny's home for the past several seasons saw him play host to his father-in-law and three neighborhood friends to watch ABC Television's presentation of *Monday Night Football*. On December 8th 1980, the game featured a match-up between the New England Patriots and the Miami Dolphins. The game was tied 13-13 with less than two minutes left in regulation time. New England's placekicker, John Smith, was about to attempt a twenty-four yard field goal to win the game. New England let the clock run down to three seconds before calling timeout. It was a tense moment on and off the field as the telecast went to a commercial break.

"Twenty-four yards, it's a lock. New England is a winner." Kenny's father-in-law Gilbert, an older gray-haired man in his sixties pronounced from his spot in an easy chair across the room.

"No – no Pop, don't be so sure," Kenny disagreed. He and two others sat on the sofa. Kenny obviously had his money on Miami. "This guy can be erratic."

♫♫♫♫♫

In the broadcast booth of the Orange Bowl in Miami, Florida, sportscasters Frank Gifford and Howard Cosell received a news item of great importance. Cosell did not want to interrupt the play-by-play at such a crucial point in the game, Gifford felt differently. "You know you gotta do it...this is gonna shake up the whole world."

"Alright," Cosell relented, "I'll get it in."

Back on camera, with Smith trotting onto the field, Cosell told millions of viewers, "An unspeakable tragedy, confirmed to us by ABC News in New York City: John Lennon, outside of his apartment building on the west side of New York – the most famous perhaps of all the Beatles. Shot twice in the back, rushed to Roosevelt Hospital – dead on arrival." He paused. "Hard to go back to the game after that bit of news."

"Indeed it is," Gifford agreed.

Smith missed the field goal.

♫ ♫ ♫ ♫ ♫

No cheers went up in the Liebermann living room. The five men sat stunned staring at the TV and the wild pandemonium going on in Miami. Fans had apparently not heard the news. Jeannie had made her way into the living room. Kenny stood and looked at her.

"Did they just say John Lennon was shot?" she asked quietly.

"Yeah," Kenny answered. "They say he's dead."

The game went into overtime with Miami winning 16-13. To many, like those in the Liebermann home, that outcome no longer mattered.

♫ ♫ ♫ ♫ ♫

It was an unusually mild December day in New York outside the Dakota, a co-op apartment building on the corner of 72nd Street and Central Park West.

John Lennon and Yoko Ono sublet an apartment there since 1973. It wasn't unusual for members of the media or fans to gather outside in the hope of catching a glimpse of the former Beatle, or even get an autograph.

Some days before, Paul Goresh, a young fan and amateur photographer left a copy of *A Spaniard in the Works*, a collection of poems and sketches Lennon wrote in 1965 at the building. He stopped by every day since to see if John signed it. On this morning, Goresh arrived and exchanged words with a strange young man standing on the opposite side of the building's archway. The man wore a fur hat and a long overcoat with a fur collar. He also carried a copy of Lennon's new LP "Double Fantasy" under his arm. Goresh went into the lobby where he met Lennon who promised to sign his book later in the day.

In the afternoon, Goresh and the strange young man still stood on opposite sides of the archway when the Lennons left the building. John reminded Goresh to pick up his signed book and then noticed the young man in the overcoat approaching him with the LP.

"Do you want that signed?" John asked.

The young man didn't say a word, but simply nodded and handed the record to Lennon who autographed it and gave it back asking, "Is there anything else you want?" Again, the boy just nodded and backed away. Goresh snapped a picture of the event.

At about 10pm, John and Yoko arrived home. They got out of their car and headed toward the lobby. Lennon again nodded at the man in the overcoat. Once they walked past him, the man drew a .38 caliber revolver from his pocket and fired five shots at the rock star. Four hollow point bullets hit John in the torso and he collapsed. His assailant made no attempt to escape. The night doorman, Jose Perdomo, disarmed the gunman and detained him.

Within minutes, police units from the 20th Precinct arrived on the scene. They recognized their victim and that there was no time to wait for an ambulance. Two patrolmen carried Lennon's body to a squad car. Another unit gathered up Ono. Both vehicles raced to nearby Roosevelt Hospital. Other officers took the suspect into custody.

When police arrived at the hospital, Doctor Stephan Lynn who was on duty in the emergency room, helped place

Lennon's unresponsive body on a gurney. The doctor prepped for emergency surgery. He examined his patient and found that all blood vessels to and from John's heart had been destroyed. For a time, Doctor Lynn held the singer's heart in his hand and performed manual compression in a last ditch effort to save him.

It was no use. John Lennon was pronounced dead.

Just a few yards away, Alan Weiss, a young reporter for ABC News awaited treatment. Earlier that evening, Weiss had been involved in a motorcycle accident in Central Park. He was at Roosevelt Hospital with minor injuries. He overheard police officers saying that Lennon had been shot, and then soon after, he recognized Yoko Ono overcome with grief. Weiss knew he had to get to a telephone.

He called the ABC news desk and told them what he knew. The executives were faced with the decision on whether or not to break in on the telecast of the football game. Someone reached out to Roone Arledge, the head of ABC Sports. He told them to call the broadcast booth in Miami and let the sportscasters deliver the news to the television audience.

Lennon's killer, later identified as Mark David Chapman, was a deeply religious yet troubled and disturbed young man. He viewed Lennon as a phony who wrote song lyrics saying that there was no heaven or hell. He made up his mind to travel from his home in Hawaii to New York City for the sole purpose of killing the former Beatle.

John's remains were cremated at Ferncliff Cemetery in Westchester County. There was no funeral.

The nightly crowds chanting outside the Dakota disturbed Ono. She made a public appeal and asked fans worldwide to convene on Sunday, December 14th for a ten-minute silent vigil.

A crowd of over 200,000 people, young and old, gathered at the band shell in Central Park for the observance.

At precisely 2pm all singing and recorded music stopped. During the ten minute vigil, every radio station in New York City ceased broadcasting.

Chapter Thirty:
"Sweet Sixteen"

Inauguration Day 1981, was cloudy with temperatures unusually mild for a mid-January Washington morning. Perhaps one of the darkest clouds over the festivities was one of doubt and uncertainty. Days before, officials completed negotiations for the release of the 52 hostages still held in Iran. The government of the Ayatollah refused to negotiate directly with the US, but agreed to deal with Algeria as an intermediary. Many viewed this as a deliberate action on the part of Iran to further punish and embarrass the Carter administration.

In return for the hostages, the United States released almost eight billion dollars in assets frozen since the takeover 444 days earlier. The process was slow and met with many delays. Lame duck President Jimmy Carter wanted desperately to have the issue resolved before Ronald Reagan took the oath of office.

"Are the hostages out?" ABC News White House correspondent Sam Donaldson asked Carter as he quickly followed President-Elect Reagan onto the Inaugural platform.

"Can't say yet," Carter curtly replied without a glance. He sat in the background during the transfer of authority. He was hurt and disappointed that the hostages remained in Tehran.

Later, at a luncheon in the statuary hall of the Capitol Building, Ronald Reagan made the official announcement. The hostages were in the air and on their way to West Germany. Reagan asked Carter to fly to Wiesbaden and act as his emissary in greeting the hostages. He did so the next day.

♫ ♫ ♫ ♫ ♫

The occasion of Danielle's sixteenth birthday was celebrated in the main ballroom of the Rye Country Club.

Joseph owed his membership to his standing in the community and his philanthropic efforts for the town.

The Siena Restaurant, a favorite location on Boston Post Road, catered the party. Johnny Maestro and the Brooklyn Bridge, a popular band since 1968 supplied the entertainment. In the fifties, Maestro sang lead with a street corner group know as the Crests. They had a string of hit records. None was more popular than "Sixteen Candles," a ballad from 1958. By this time, the Brooklyn Bridge had incorporated some of the Crest's songs into their act.

Many girls her age would have thought dancing to a song like this with their father as rather lame, but not Danielle. She relished the moment. She wore a long shimmering blue gown and her hair was up in a French knot with ringlets framing her face. Janet applied light make-up around her eyes. She looked so grown up.

A local rock band from her school played alternate sets of music more to the tastes of Danielle's friends. They called themselves Leapfrog. They did a creditable job covering current hits of the day like "Jesse's Girl," "Rock This Town," and a patriotic monster hit from Neil Diamond, "America."

At the moment, Trish Miller, Danielle's classmate, sat at the Rabinowitz table chirping in Joseph's ear about the talents of her boyfriend Eddie, singing lead with Leapfrog.

"They are really good, aren't they Mr. Rabinowitz?" she asked excitedly.

"Yes they are," he answered.

Danielle, sitting next to Trish, enjoyed watching her dad squirm under the constant barrage of teenage questioning. Janet stifled a smile of her own by putting her hand to her face.

Trish wouldn't let up. "And if you still had a record company, you might even sign them up?"

"Well," Joseph began, "I no longer have a record company." Then after thinking for a moment, "I'll tell you what. This summer we're expanding our entertainment schedule at Playland to include Wednesday nights. Now, if you can get all the guys parents to sign permission slips, I'll hire them to do every other Wednesday this summer. How's that?"

"You will?" Trish squealed with glee jumping out of her chair. "Omigod!" She bounced at Joseph and hugged him tightly. "Oh, thank you Mr. Rabinowitz. I gotta go tell Eddie. C'mon Dani, lets find him."

Danielle patted Joseph on his back as she whizzed past him.

"Your next *comet*?" Janet asked with a smile, a reference to the old days when each new discovery would lead them in a new direction.

"No, no," Joseph insisted, "I'm not chasing comets anymore."

He recalled a time when something like this would cause him to contact his old partner Leo Klein. Leo would then undoubtedly brand the new enterprise as "a fad," but then jump in with both feet just because his faith in Joseph superseded logical thought.

Leo was gone now. He suffered a severe heart attack early in eighty-one and died in the spring. His memorial drew hundreds of mourners from the secular, business and music worlds, Joseph and Janet among them. The loss of such a close friend and the man who staked him to everything was difficult to absorb.

Aside from his father, and perhaps Chanticleer, Joseph judged Leo to be the most influential man in his life. Without his trust and support there would have been no record company, no career and fame, no reunion concert, none of it. Perhaps that was why Joseph now felt it was his responsibility to help young musicians and singers whenever he could. But Leapfrog? *Why not?*

Chapter Thirty-One:
"The Cover of Rolling Stone"

Janet's book *The Holy Land* became a worldwide best seller. One photograph in particular titled "Best of Both Worlds" won the prestigious Graham-Crimmins Award for Outstanding Achievement in Photography in 1981. The photo depicted a group of young Arab boys selling trinkets to an elderly Jewish couple in a market outside Tel-Aviv. In addition to the $20,000.00 cash award, her work was selected for exhibition at the Corcoran Gallery in Washington DC. The Rabinowitz family enjoyed their time in the nation's capital. Danielle got to wear her long pretty gown for a second time at the black-tie dinner held in her mother's honor.

Early in 1982, Janet was asked to take a portrait photograph of the rock band Journey for the cover of *Rolling Stone* magazine. Since 1967, the magazine had been published bi-monthly by Jann Wenner and Ralph Gleason. It soon became *the* major publication for music and politics aimed directly at the youth market. The first issue from November 9th 1967 featured a photo of John Lennon from the motion picture *How I Won the War*. Some other covers became legendary, owing to the brilliant work of photographers like Baron Wolman and Annie Leibovitz. This opportunity provided another proud moment in Janet's career.

♪♪♪♪♪

The shopping district along Morris Park Avenue in the Bronx provided for the needs of the large number of residents living in the homes and apartment buildings of the area. Specialty stores were abundant. Spatafora's sold the finest quality cuts of beef, pork, lamb and veal. Skilled father and son butchers cut up chickens to the specific needs of housewives like Barbara Seracino and countless others.

Genarro's Bakery was the place to go for fresh rolls and

buns for Sunday mornings after Mass, or for butter-cream birthday cakes when the occasions arose. The Morris Park Fruit Store brought in a wide variety of fresh fruit and vegetables from the Hunt's Point Market on a daily basis. Staples like canned goods, cleaning products, milk, butter and such, were purchased from Barbara's favorite place to shop, the Grand Union Supermarket.

It wasn't uncommon for her to run into any number of people she knew from the neighborhood as she shopped. She enjoyed pausing in the middle of an aisle to chat for a few minutes. However, one particular encounter was most uncommon and darn near jolting.

With her head turned, Barbara perused the shelves looking for her favorite brand of tomato sauce. Her metal shopping cart bumped the front of another headed in the opposite direction. When she looked up to apologize, the face she saw shocked her.

It was Jimmy Stannic.

She hadn't seen him in a while. He looked as though he put on weight, at least twenty pounds. He was bald except for some hair on either side over his ears and around the back of his head.

"Hey lady watch where you're going?" he joked with a broad smile. "We'll have to exchange insurance information."

"Jimmy? You're a bit out of your area, aren't you?"

It bothered Jimmy that she didn't seem happy to see him. "Not really. I report to the transit yard right up here off Eastchester Road."

Despite his answer, Barbara was well aware of a Grand Union store within walking distance of the project where Jimmy lived. A quick glance at the sparse contents of his shopping cart didn't dispel her curiosity. A loaf of white bread, a container of milk and a can of pork and beans…nothing he couldn't buy in Throggs Neck.

"How have you been Jimmy?" she asked.

"I've been fine. How about you guys?"

"Good…good. My son Steven got married last month."

"Wow. Guess that means you'll be a grandmother soon?"

Barbara didn't take that as a compliment. "I guess maybe, I don't know."

"You sure have a lot of stuff there."

"Yeah, I like to stock up so I only have to come in here once a week."

Jimmy knew this. "If you want, I can help you home…"

His suggestion made her a bit uneasy. "No, that's okay. I have our station wagon outside and my daughter is waiting for me. But it was good seeing you again Jimmy." As Barbara tried to maneuver her shopping cart away from his, Jimmy appeared reluctant to let her pass.

"Yeah, you too." He moved out of her way. "Tell Johnny I said hi."

"I will," she said without looking at him.

Jimmy was angry. He hurried his cart to the front of the store and with a loud bang slammed it into the side of a checkout counter. Jimmy stormed out of the Grand Union without his groceries.

On the short ride home, Barbara looked into the rearview mirror several times to see if Jimmy followed. She didn't understand why she felt so threatened, but she was. Perhaps it was seeing him shopping in her neighborhood? Asking if he could drive her home? Or maybe it was just the way he looked at her?

She considered telling Johnny about the incident, but thought better of it. He had to fly to Florida in two days. The Du-Kanes would be out of town for three weeks headlining a series of oldies shows through the Sunshine State. Surely she was safe at home. Just in case, she'd make sure she kept Jeanne Liebermann close and have Steven and Pam over for dinner a few times.

Chapter Thirty-Two:
"The Big Bang"

Throughout the twentieth century, villains in the field of science fiction wielded weapons emanating deadly beams of light. Often described as "death rays," these beams were capable of melting the thickest armor and pulverizing the human form.

In 1959, Bell Laboratories received a patent for a process to harness beams of light called Lasers, an acronym for Light Amplification by Stimulated Emission of Radiation. The applications of laser technology proved vast and included, industrial, medical, military, environmental and consumer electronics.

In the late sixties, a scientist named James Russell designed the first optical sound recording system. It was comprised of a photosensitive platter 4.7 inches in diameter around a 15mm center hole. The disc was embedded with "light and dark bits," similar to the binary code system of 0's and 1's used to represent text in computer language. The disc held 80 minutes of uncompressed audio data. Their compact size led to the name Compact Disc, or CD.

The playback unit contained a semi-conductor laser beam, reading the data from beneath the disc which rotated at a speed of about 500RPM. Since the laser read the information from the inside outward, the disc slowed down to about 200 RPM as it neared the end. The disc itself was three-layered. The bottom layer, made of polycarbonate contained the encoded data. A thin layer of aluminum made the disc reflective and a layer of protective lacquer followed. The label was printed on the lacquer by offset or screen printing. The finished product resulted in a durable storage system with enhanced quality sound even though there was actually no music at all on a CD. Instead, it is only a long list of numbers.

It would be nearly a decade before the Sony Corporation and Philips Electronics purchased the patent and entered into a joint agreement to manufacture CDs. Though both companies had confidence in the success of the new technology, several factors accounted for their wait and see attitude. For one thing, component CD players were expensive, costing nearly a thousand dollars in their first design. Another factor was the attitude exhibited by record companies. The short-lived success of the eight-track tape system made executives at Columbia, Capitol and RCA reluctant to embrace yet another new format that would force them to duplicate their entire inventory. But the time had come and CDs were on their way to mass production.

The manufacturing process was similar to that of a vinyl record. After a master disc was burned, "stamper" molds were created. During the electroplating process, liquefied polycarbonate was injected into a mold and thousands of CDs were then pressed from those.

The new format required new packaging. Paper and cardboard sleeves were quickly rejected. A Philips' engineer named Peter Doodson came up with a three-piece hinged plastic design containing a media tray with a grooved out section that gripped the disc through the center hole. The case could also accommodate a folded front and back cover for printed information and liner notes. Its design proved to work so perfectly it was dubbed the Jewel Case.

The introduction of the compact disc was viewed as the "Big Bang" in the audio world.

Chapter Thirty-Three:
"Ride Sally Ride"

Danielle enjoyed her time as an upperclassman at Rye High School. Thanks to Jacki and Brian, the escapade involving Amadeus at Beacon Theatre became legendary. She was viewed as something of a rebel, a reputation she freely embraced. Going into her junior year, more of the boys at school began to notice her developing figure. While certainly not cheerleader caliber, she now filled out her sweaters well and her legs were quite shapely. She once heard two boys talking in a corridor about how she had a neat seat. This was an off-handed compliment to be sure, but one Danielle accepted.

She went to her senior prom with a boy named Kevin, the third one to ask her. It wasn't that she didn't like the other two. Ryan was a hunk, blonde haired and blue eyed the star pitcher on the school's baseball team. David was more the studious type, average looking, a sense of humor and a good dancer. Yet, she held out and waited for Kevin. She thought of him as cute, kind of skinny with dark framed glasses reminding her of pictures she saw of the singer Buddy Holly. As President of the Science Club, Kevin was, in a word, *interesting.* She enjoyed listening to his dissertations on outer space. They became good friends. Sometimes they ate lunch alone together, or met after school and walked along the boardwalk or on the asphalt paths at the periphery of Rye Playland.

"President Reagan is talking about setting up a defense system in space," Kevin would tell her. "So that if we're ever attacked we can shoot down enemy missiles before they ever reach us."

He was speaking of the Strategic Defense Initiative, or SDI. Though only in its planning stages, the system could one day prove to be a major deterrent to nuclear war. There were those skeptical of the scope and cost of such a project. Some media sources called the venture, the "Star Wars Defense System," a reference to the epic science fiction movie series of the same name created by George Lucas of *American Graffiti* fame.

"You'll probably think this is silly," Kevin confided in Danielle one afternoon, "but I'd like to become an astronaut."

Her reply was most cheery, "I don't think it's silly at all. I think you'd make a terrific astronaut."

According to Kevin the region of space just beyond the earth's atmosphere was crowded with man-made satellites, communications satellites, weather satellites and spy satellites galore. All the major powers had ambitious plans to build manned space stations. The need arose for a re-usable spacecraft which could launch a crew into orbit to deliver or recover material and perform tasks ranging from deploying and repairing equipment. Then it would return to Earth in a soft landing like any ordinary aircraft.

The US accomplished this task by implementing the Space Shuttle program. Kevin expressed his keen desire to be a part of a shuttle crew.

♫ ♫ ♫ ♫ ♫

In June, Sally Ride, a thirty-two year old physicist from Encino, California, became the first American woman in space when she spent six days aboard the space shuttle Challenger. Danielle felt the need to commemorate this event in some grand way.

It was pure coincidence that the female astronaut's name was mentioned in the lyric of a song, "Mustang Sally," recorded in 1967 by Wilson Pickett. Danielle convinced three of her girlfriends to join her in an impromptu march down the main corridor at school. With their arms intertwined, and kicking their legs like a New York Radio City Rockette's chorus line, they sang at the top of their lungs, "All you gotta do is ride along Sally, ride Sally ride!"

Although a fitting tribute, school officials reprimanded the girls for their action.

Two days after the incident, Kevin asked Danielle to the prom.

She would have surrendered her virginity to Kevin had he pressed the issue, but he never did. Sometimes their walks along the boardwalk took them to the large covered wooden dock where sightseeing ferryboats delivered passengers to the amusement park. In the off-season the dock saw little foot traffic and remained pretty much deserted. It provided opportunities for kissing, groping and exploration, which the couple sometimes took advantage of. It wasn't the same as exploring outer space, but Kevin enjoyed it anyway.

Keeping in mind the circumstances of her own conception, Danielle went all the way to New Rochelle to buy a box of condoms to bring to the prom. The effort proved unnecessary. Prom night ended with a deep kiss on the Rabinowitz patio when he dropped her off.

Though nothing was said about it that night, Kevin *did* have an explanation.

"I sure like you an awful lot Dani, you know that. But I have so much work ahead of me this summer and then college in the fall. I don't think it would be fair to you if we got involved in a relationship right now."

Kevin earned a partial scholarship to the Massachusetts Institute of Technology, the first step to achieving his dream. She thought well of him for having so much respect for her. She understood, even though it hurt.

Danielle's plans for higher education were less ambitious. She enrolled at Columbia University in Morningside Heights in Manhattan, an easy commute via the New York Central Railroad. Her intentions were to get a BA degree in Liberal Arts and then switch to a business oriented program and get a job with Chanticleer Enterprises. Mid-way through her first semester, she found the distractions of the city to be too much. There were just too many parties and too many late nights at V & T's Pizzeria on Amsterdam Avenue for great pizza and beer, too many boys who weren't as respectful as her good friend Kevin. One in particular found his way to the ultimate prize of Danielle's virtue, an upperclassman named Simon. He was a political science major who literally charmed her out of her panties. When that relationship fizzled out she behaved in what she believed to be a debauched and depraved series of one night stands and unfulfilling sexual encounters. She needed a change.

♫♫♫♫♫

"I just don't wanna be a disappointment to you and dad," she told her mother after deciding to leave school.

"I'm not disappointed, and I doubt he will be either. We're fortunate to be able to offer you a good education, that's all. Ultimately the decision is yours."

"And he'll give me a job with the company?"

Janet laughed. "I'm sure he'll find something for you."

"But will I have to start at the bottom, cleaning bathrooms maybe?"

"Nothing so menial. Though, I wouldn't count on being made vice-president or anything like that." Mother and daughter hugged before Janet suggested, "Hey, what say we go and get some ice cream?"

Chapter Thirty-Four:
"New Years Rockin' Eve"

While continuing in his role as host of *American Bandstand*, a position he held since 1956, Dick Clark was nick named "America's Oldest Teenager." His business acumen saw him emerge as a media mogul. His company, Dick Clark Productions, was responsible for many shows and television specials. When ABC television lost the rights to broadcast the Grammy Awards, Clark created a new show called *The American Music Awards* with the winners selected by a poll of the music buying public.

In 1973, he became the host of an afternoon game show *The $10,000 Pyramid*. That same year he produced and hosted *New Years Rockin' Eve*, an event broadcast live from Times Square in New York. The show brought in the New Year with a lineup of musical acts performing on both coasts.

On the tenth anniversary of the show, a national magazine asked Janet to do a photo spread. She and Danielle were excited at the prospect.

♫♫♫♫♫

"C'mon Dad, why don't you come with us? It'll be so much fun," Danielle pestered Joseph.

"Being in the middle of thousands of people freezing in Times Square on New Year's Eve isn't exactly my idea of fun," Joseph defended his position.

Janet took Danielle's side in this. "Dick Clark's staff assures me they have several very warm trailers just a short way from the set and they are very comfortable. And it certainly will be fun to actually be there instead of watching it on TV."

"Well, I'll tell you what, you two be sure to wave to me and I'll let you know if I saw you on television," Joseph responded with a laugh.

"Oh Dad," Danielle complained, "you're such a party pooper."

"You surely are," her mom agreed.

🎵🎵🎵🎵🎵

New Year's Eve 1983 was cold with no precipitation expected. The magazine provided a car that picked Janet and Danielle up at the house and drove them to Times Square. Their credentials got them through the police barriers set up to keep unauthorized traffic out of the area. They were allowed to pass onto the street where ABC Television crews had their trailers and equipment prepped for their live remote broadcast.

"Mrs. Rabinowitz?" a voice nearby asked.

"Yes?" Janet looked to see a young blonde woman with a clipboard approach them.

"My name is Caroline, I'm one of Mr. Clark's assistants. If the two of you will just follow me."

Caroline guided them through a mass of people and vehicles until they arrived at a large trailer parked at the curb. Inside Dick Clark was waiting. The ever gracious and charming music icon shot his legendary smile Janet's way as he rose to greet her. "My goodness Janet, how good it is to see you again." The two embraced.

"Dick this is my daughter Danielle."

"You are quite lovely my dear."

Danielle blushed as they shook hands. Janet went on, "She's working for Joseph now as an intern with the company."

"That's wonderful. There's nothing like keeping things in the family. My wife and I were so glad when we heard you got this assignment. We love your work."

"Thank you."

"We'll leave for the make-up trailer in a few minutes. I thought it would be fun to have some pictures showing how much time it *really* takes to make me look good. *America's oldest teenager*...isn't that just the most ridiculous thing? Anyway, I'm sure all that would be terribly boring for Danielle soooo," he beamed at his next announcement, "my assistant has come up with a bit of a surprise that I think Danielle is going to like. She's bringing over this year's headliner to spend a little time with her." He then asked Danielle, "What would you say to meeting TJ Russell?"

When Janet and Danielle gaped at one another, the smile melted from Clark's face. In what seemed like the most awkward of moments, he finally got it.

"Omigod," the fingers of his hand flew up to cover his mouth. "The Teddy Boyette thing! It never registered with me. This is so embarrassing. I'm so sorry Janet. I'll try to stop..."

It was too late. At that very moment, the door to the trailer opened and Caroline entered just ahead of TJ Russell. She was downright bubbly in her introduction.

"TJ, I'd like you to meet Janet Rabinowitz and her daughter Danielle."

The young man's reaction was instantaneous, leaving only Caroline out of the loop. He broke the icy silence by extending his hand to Janet. "Mrs. Rabinowitz."

"Hello," Janet replied with a limp handshake. Danielle just nodded his way and averted eye contact though she felt certain he couldn't possibly remember her. The singer hadn't changed much since the last time she'd seen him. He was now clean shaven and his hair less unruly.

"I'm glad I got the chance to meet you finally," TJ said. "When your husband and I first met, I don't think we got off on the right foot."

Janet wanted to hear more, but Clark interrupted. "We really have to hurry things along. We're on a tight schedule. Janet if you'll come with me? Caroline, will you see if Danielle and TJ would like any refreshments?"

"Are you gonna be okay here?" Janet asked her daughter.

"Yeah, I'm fine."

"I'll be back as soon as I can," her mom told her before picking up her camera gear. Dick Clark ushered her out of the trailer. Danielle took a seat in a chair.

"Do you think I could get a cup of coffee?" TJ asked Caroline. "Black, two sugars."

"Yeah sure, no problem. How about you Danielle?"

"No thanks. I'm good."

"I'll be back in a little bit." Caroline didn't understand why, but she was happy to get out of there. Once they were alone, TJ had a closer look at Danielle.

"Have we met?" he asked.

She thought about lying, then decided not to. "You once called me a snot nosed kid."

It took a while for a glimmer of recollection to cross his face. "The Beacon? That was what...four years ago? Let's see, you were supposed to be Artie Franklin's granddaughter, or something that night? Tell me, is Mrs. Rabinowitz really your mother?"

Danielle didn't appreciate his sarcasm, but understood it. "Grand *niece,* I said I was his grand niece. But, yes she is my mother and Joseph Rabinowitz is my father."

"That explains a lot. I meant what I said before about your father and me."

"We know all about that," Danielle said sternly.

"You know, I seem to recall you didn't have a very high opinion of me either."

"I called you an obnoxious asshole."

TJ chuckled. "I often wondered something. Did you go to all that trouble to bribe your way backstage that night just to insult me?"

Once again, a lie would be meaner than the truth. She settled on the truth.

"No I actually *liked* Amadeus. I thought they had a good sound. But when I saw the way you talked to the rest of the guys, I remembered all the crappy things you said about

Teddy Boyette. I decided to tell you what I thought about you right then and there."

"You're a damn kid," he dismissed her out of hand. "What the Hell do you know about Teddy Boyette?"

"I know as much as you. And *nobody* knows more than my mom and dad."

"I'd have to disagree with you there. I think my mom knew him pretty well."

"You know, none of it matters anyway. Your mom is gone. Teddy is gone. It all comes down to *what* people choose to believe. Why should *anyone* believe either one of us? After all we're both bastards aren't we?"

Her remark stunned him. Danielle fought back tears and looked away. TJ realized that what she said was as damning an insult as she could possibly come up with, damning to him and damning to her.

After composing herself, she had more to say, "My real father was a drug addict. I read a lot of stories about the bad things other people said he did. But I don't remember the bad things. I remember things like sitting alone with him while he played his guitar and sang to me. I guess that's really all I *want* to remember. Do you, way deep down in your heart, really believe that Teddy Boyette was really your father?"

"Yes I do," TJ replied without hesitation. "Why?"

"Because If I didn't believe it that would make my mama a liar. And I'd rather not think about her in that way. If that's okay with you?"

In the moment of utter silence that followed, a knock came upon the trailer door.

"What is it?" TJ called out.

The door opened slightly and Caroline peeked in. Deciding that the coast was clear she stepped inside. "I have your coffee."

TJ told her, "I think I'll take that to go." He took the paper cup from her hand and said to Danielle, "Tell your mother it *was* a pleasure to meet her."

Seconds later, he was gone.

"Are you okay?" Caroline asked.

Danielle simply nodded.

The remainder of the evening went well. They watched the New Year Ball drop while standing on the elevated platform overlooking the huge throng of people gathered in Times Square. Danielle had another opportunity to admire her mom at work. They opted out of the after-show party and bid good-bye to their host in his trailer.

In the car back to Westchester, her mom told her, "Dick and I were hysterical about that TJ thing. Was everything okay after I left?" When Danielle simply shrugged, Janet pressed her. "Dani did something happen?"

"Nah, it was awkward, that's all. He's an asshole, what more can I say?" After a pause she asked, "Do you think Dad will be sorry he didn't tag along?"

Janet laughed. "Joseph is not going to believe this."

"Probably not."

She sat quietly for the rest of the way. TJ's remark about his mother resonated in her. It was as though she could suddenly see the situation from his side. It must have been painful that everyone doubted him and questioned his mother's integrity, believing she kept silent because she was being paid off. He distanced himself so far from Teddy's legacy and became a success based on his own talent. There was no question her feelings were now changing, softening to the point, where she felt maybe he wasn't such a bad guy after all.

Chapter Thirty-Five:
"Shira"

In the years since returning from Israel, Danielle and Shira Bar-On exchanged letters on a regular basis. Both of them shared great joy when the hostage crisis in Iran came to an end. Danielle's letters were lighthearted and almost frivolous. She told her far-away pen pal about the important events in her life, like her romance with Kevin and her wild failed college experience. She also boasted about the new job she now had with her father's company. Shira's pages took on a more somber tone.

Two recent terrorist attacks in nearby Lebanon took a huge toll in lives. A suicide car bombing at the US Embassy in Beirut killed over 60 Americans. Three hundred more died in October when two suicide bombers drove their vehicles into a military barracks.

Personal tragedy struck in November 1983 when the Israeli Defense Force Headquarters in Tyre was bombed killing more than sixty. According to her letter, one of Shira's closest friends from her time in the military was among the dead.

Just after the holidays, Shira wrote to Danielle once again. This correspondence was different and more a cryptic note than a letter.

> Dani:
> There's no need to respond to this. I don't know if a letter would ever catch up with me. I'm going away for a short time. A lot has happened and I've much to consider. I will be in touch with you, I promise.
> Much Love,
> Shira

Then, nearly eight months later, wonderful news reached Danielle. Shira was coming to America.

♫♫♫♫♫

Shira provided rather sketchy details. Apparently she accepted a job with the AJC. The American Jewish Council was a philanthropic organization with its headquarters on 1st Avenue in Manhattan, not far from the United Nations building.

Her arrival coincided with the Labor Day holiday weekend in September. Shira accepted the invitation to spend her first weekend in America with Danielle and her family. Joseph arranged for a car to bring her to Rye.

The reunion between the two friends outside the house was warm and affectionate as they embraced at the curb. Shira felt solid in her arms and Danielle was surprised to see that she had cut her hair in a short pageboy style. She was tanned evenly on her face and neck and dressed rather formally in a black pant-suit and button down white blouse.

Janet greeted Shira in much the same way. As she was introduced to Joseph they exchanged a strong handshake.

"Mr. Rabinowitz," Shira said with great respect, "it's an honor to meet you. Dani has told me so much about you."

"I've heard a lot about you too. Welcome to America."

"Oh thank you sir."

"It'll be Joseph, or Joe, if you don't mind," he told the young woman.

"He prefers Joseph," Dani said.

"Then, Joseph it will be."

"Come on," Danielle said excitedly, "let me show you my place."

She took Shira around to the side of the house through a wooden gate that led to a large back yard. The Rabinowitz's home featured an in-ground swimming pool and a small pool house. For Danielle's eighteenth birthday, Joseph had the pool house renovated with a kitchenette and bathroom, giving his daughter what amounted to her own private apartment.

As they entered the apartment, Shira was happy to see the silver Mezuzah, her parting gift to Danielle when she came home from Israel, affixed to the right side of the front doorpost. Inside, her space was quite cozy. She had a four-poster brass bed inhabited by plush pillows and an array of stuffed animals. There was a dresser on one wall and a desk opposite it. She had a TV and small table and chairs. In typical young adult fashion, she had several posters on her walls. In addition to a crinkled and faded KISS poster, there was one of Don Mattingly. The rookie first baseman of the New York Yankees looked quite imposing in his batting stance.

"It's perfect for me," Danielle told her friend. "You're going to be staying in one of the guest rooms in the house. But we can hang out in here whenever we want."

"That's lovely."

Later, Shira enjoyed her first American barbecue replete with grilled hamburgers, hot dogs and chicken. There was also corn on the cob, potato salad and cole slaw. They sat around talking as sunset approached.

"Shira, Dani tells me the Council provides for your lodging as well?" Janet asked.

"Yes, a small studio apartment in the Tudor City complex on First Avenue." Shira giggled as she went on. "Actually, it's not much bigger than Dani's little nest here."

Joseph was impressed. "Tudor City is really swanky. That must be quite a job."

Shira paused for a moment before commenting, "I'm not supposed to say much about it. Since you and your family are the only people I know in America, I feel I can trust you."

"Of course you can sweetheart," Janet assured her.

"It's really more of a posting than it is a job." She looked Danielle's way. "As I told you in my letters, I lost a very close friend in the recent bombings." She went back to addressing everyone. "Working in the hotel suddenly seemed shallow and empty. I needed to do something that mattered for my country. I went back into the military. I joined Mossad."

"The Israeli intelligence agency?" Joseph asked.

"A branch of it actually, the Shin Bet. Do you know it?"

"No," Joseph replied.

"It's primarily for internal security. We report directly to the Prime Minister. The woman I work for at the Council is the wife of a highly placed minister in our government. I'm responsible for her safety while she's at work."

"Security?" Janet commented. "That sounds dangerous."

Shira was quick to respond, "We're in America... New York. How dangerous can it be?"

"You're kidding right?" Danielle remarked with her mouth wide open.

When everyone else at the table laughed, she realized her friend poked fun at her. "I went through six months of extensive training. I feel I can handle myself most adequately."

"Do you carry a gun?" Danielle asked.

"Yes, but it's a small one."

As the sun dipped below the horizon, a series of loud bangs broke the silence. Off in the distance, flashes of light appeared in the darkening sky. It surprised everyone, but startled Shira the most. She spun around then quickly calmed down.

"I'm sorry," she explained, "that gave me a jolt."

"That's just fireworks," Danielle explained, "from the amusement park. It's the end of summer celebration. Tomorrow night my dad is putting on a show at the band stand. It's gonna be great fun. They'll be lots of cute guys there. We'll have a blast. I can't wait."

"It sounds like great fun," Shira said with a broad smile.

After tidying up the patio, the girls went into the house

leaving Joseph and Janet alone.

"She's quite a young woman," Joseph said.

"Yes, she is…very brave…very dedicated. Did you see the way she reacted to the fireworks?"

"Yes," Joseph said with a nod, "in her part of the world, hearing something like that has an entirely different meaning."

"I hope Dani can help her assimilate."

Early the next day, Danielle bounced down the staircase to find her mother. Shira followed sheepishly.

"Mom, we have a fashion emergency. I was helping Shira pick out an outfit for today and look at her. All she brought with her is this army khaki thing and an ugly blouse."

"Please Dani," Shira pleaded. "You're embarrassing me."

"Better you're embarrassed now than later in front of all my friends. That set may be okay in Tel Aviv, but at Rye Playland it's not gonna work."

"I'm sorry, Mrs. Rabinowitz, at some things I'm not very with-it."

"That's quite alright dear. Dani is overreacting."

"Mom…I'm not overreacting. We have to do something. None of *my* things will fit her."

Janet had a plan. "We have time. The mall is open. We can go and get a few things."

"Please no. I don't want to put you out." Shira looked away.

"Nonsense. Just some shorts and a couple of tops."

Danielle hugged her friend tightly. "See, I told you. My mom always saves the day.

♪♪♪♪♪

The day of the "Last Summer Bash" at Playland was a

whirlwind of excitement for everyone. Danielle and Shira, now decked out in fashionable shorts and a shoestring blouse, laughed their way through the amusement park. They rode the Grand Carousel, the Dragon Coaster and other attractions, ate cotton candy and caramel apples. Danielle had a great time introducing her Middle Eastern visitor to her friends and former schoolmates.

At nightfall, they headed to the main stage area on the north side of the park near Mansuring Lake. They joined a large crowd to hear the performance of the Duprees, another of the finer vocal groups from the mid-sixties. By applying their doo-wop harmonies to older big band tunes, they had huge success with songs like "You Belong to Me," "My Own True Love," and "Have You Heard." The crowd loved them. Afterward, a local band took the stage and kept younger fans on their feet until closing time. Danielle danced several times with boys she knew. Shira declined every invitation to the dance floor.

The two girls walked home. Neither of them felt tired and didn't want the night to end.

"Hey," Danielle offered in a mischievous hush, "go change real quick and come meet me in my place."

"Okay," Shira whispered.

Once inside, Danielle hurriedly stripped out of her top, shorts and bra and threw a New York Yankees t-shirt over her head. She moved to her bed and tossed aside the stuffed animals, before fluffing two pillows and throwing a light summer top sheet down the length of the bed to make for a comfy spot. A soft knock came upon her door.

"Come in," she said.

Her attention was drawn to the figure of Shira standing in the doorway. She was wearing a sheer lime green silk nightie. Her nipples and the dark patch of her pubic area easily discernible beneath the thin fabric.

"Wow, that's pretty sexy," Danielle remarked.

"Well, I'm glad to see you don't also hate my taste in

underwear," Shira kidded.

They hopped into opposite sides of the bed. Danielle propped two pillows behind her head and leaned back. Shira did the same.

"How come you didn't dance with any of those boys who asked you? That Scott is a real hunk."

Shira changed position to look her friend in the eye. "Dani, you must understand, all this is still rather overwhelming to me. This country, this culture, the way you Americans do things...it's going to take some getting used to."

Danielle reached around and twirled an end of Shira's hair in her hand. "Why did you cut your hair?"

"It seemed wise since I was back in the military, out in the middle of the desert. It's more comfortable this way."

"Will you let it grow back?"

Shira leaned up and turned. "Why, don't you like it?

Their faces were inches apart. Their eyes locked. Shira moved even closer and kissed Danielle softly yet firmly on the mouth. When she probed with her tongue, her friend recoiled. Shira sat up as though shot.

"That was most inappropriate. Please Dani, forgive me?"

"I uh...I just wasn't expecting..."

"Dani, I'm gay."

Danielle responded with the only word that came to mind, "Oh."

Feeling the need to explain, Shira began with deep emotion. "In my first stint in the army, I became close friends with the only other girl my age in our unit. Her name was Rebecca. She was much more suited to military life than I. The training was hard. We were both frightened, afraid to go to war, afraid to die. We became lovers and we did not hide the fact." She relaxed her position and put her head against Danielle's shoulder before continuing. "One night while I was on guard duty, I heard a noise. I was petrified. I called out and challenged for the password but no one answered. Then I was relieved to see that it was just three young boys from my unit." She squeezed Danielle's arms tightly, began sobbing and shaking. "They were drunk and rowdy. One of them grabbed hold of me and knocked me down. The others laughed. They got me to my feet and one of them told me that they were going to show me *how a woman's body was supposed to be used*. All three had their way with me." Shira relaxed a bit and looked up at Danielle. "I haven't been able to let a man touch me since."

"Oh my God Shira." Danielle comforted her friend. She reached up and wiped at the tears in Shira's eyes. "What a terrible thing to endure."

"I better go," Shira whispered.

"No stay. I want you to."

Danielle leaned in and kissed her. This time she did not deny Shira's tongue and responded with equal passion. Shira reached for Danielle's hand moving it to her own breast. She let out a hushed moan as Danielle squeezed her nipple.

♫♫♫♫♫

There was a noticeable difference in Danielle's behavior in the days after Shira left for the city. Janet made no mention of it until laundry day when they separated clothes and she discovered a pair of khaki shorts in the pile. She held them up.

"These are Shira's aren't they?"

"Yeah. That's her idea of a joke. She said if I wore them around the house a couple of times I might get to like them."

Janet laughed. Danielle didn't seem to think it was funny. "You can throw them out if you like."

"I will not throw them out. You can return them the next time you see her."

"Mom, about Shira…"

"Sweetheart," her mother interrupted, "you're going to have to give Shira some time to adjust. She's from a much different culture. She needs *time*."

"I know. That's what she says so too."

Janet pressed, "Is there something else you wanted to tell me?"

Danielle simply shook her head.

Chapter Thirty-Six:
"Goofy"

Though they talked on the phone every day, three weeks passed before Danielle and Shira made plans for a weekend visit to Shira's apartment in the city. They agreed on the date and talked excitedly on some of the things Shira wanted to see and do. Visiting the Statue of Liberty and the Empire State Building were high on the list. Neither of them spoke of the intimacy they shared in Rye.

Danielle traveled light throwing enough clothing for a two-day stay into a backpack. She boarded a commuter train one Friday afternoon heading to Grand Central Station. Shira met her at the Lexington Avenue entrance. They embraced warmly and then strolled along 42nd Street, stopping a time or two to peek into a store window. At 2nd Avenue, they climbed the staircase to the residential skyscraper complex known as Tudor City. The neo-gothic structures stood on a granite cliff overlooking 1st Avenue. Almost a city within a city, it featured parks, playgrounds its own pharmacy, beauty salon, gourmet deli, laundry and dry cleaners.

Shira's fourteenth floor studio apartment was accessible by a small elevator. At a mere three-hundred and twenty square feet, the interior was tight as well. She had a small kitchenette area. A full-sized Murphy bed folded into a closet on one wall when not in use. That left room for a table and chairs and a loveseat big enough for two.

"It's so very tiny I know," Shira said almost apologetically as they entered, "but I don't need much more. And the price is right. The Council pays for it all, even utilities."

"Wow." Danielle took it all in. "I think it's cute...cozy. Where's your TV?"

"I don't watch much TV Dani."

"Oh. Well, like I said, cozy."

"I *do* have a radio though if you'd like to listen to some

music?"

"No. That's okay."

"I'll start dinner. It'll take awhile."

"I'll help."

Shira broiled two small pieces of fish in perfect portions for each of them. She steamed some vegetables while Danielle mixed a salad and then made a tasty dressing.

When they finished eating Shira asked, "Did you have enough? I'm not used to cooking for company."

"It was plenty. The fish was delicious."

"I'm glad you liked it. It's an old Jewish recipe of my mother's."

"My mom learned Jewish cooking from my Gramma Myra. She lives in Florida. You two would get along great." Danielle's eyes brightened with an idea. "Hey, we can go visit her, you and me, when you get your vacation."

Shira laughed. "My goodness Dani, I just got this job. I doubt I'll be entitled to any kind of vacation for at least a year."

"That's okay," she wouldn't be deterred. "It's better if we go in the winter time anyway when it gets cold and snows here."

Shira pouted. "Aw, but Dani, I was rather looking forward to the cold weather. I've never really seen snow before."

"Never seen snow? Holy smoke!" The two of them laughed.

"I think I'd love to learn to ski."

"Skiing is cool...and snowmobiling...snowmobiling is such fun. My parents and I go up to the Poconos in Pennsylvania every winter. You can come too."

Shira smiled. "Or *we* could go, just the two of us." When Danielle didn't respond Shira changed the subject. "I've yet to find a good vegetable market in the neighborhood."

"We'll find one tomorrow. We'll explore everywhere."

"I have subway and bus maps. But eventually, I think

I'd like to get a bicycle."

"Oh, that's so neat. I'll bet lots of people around here go places by bike."

With the dishes done, the two girls relaxed side by side on the loveseat. Shira brought out a tattered photo album. She opened it up across her lap.

"I didn't know most of the people in these pictures. Many were killed in the camps."

"That's the way it was with Joseph's family too. Were your parents in...the camps?"

"No. They lived in Spain when the Nazis came to power." She turned the page. Her somber expression changed. She moved the album to allow her friend a closer look. "These are my parents."

Danielle looked at a photograph of a loving couple sitting close together on a park bench. Shira's father had his arm around her mother. They were cheek to cheek.

"They look really happy," Danielle commented.

Shira took the album back and lingered on the page, running the flat of her hand across the photo. "I was told it was taken the day before they immigrated to Palestine. It was an exciting time for them...the beginning of a new life in a new land."

"Like *you're* doing now?"

"Yes, I suppose you *could* say that." Shira flipped ahead several pages. Almost to the end, she stopped at a page holding just two pictures. "And this...this is Rebecca." Once again she handed the album over to her friend. Shira's close friend Rebecca was truly beautiful. Olive skin with dark features, she was taller than Shira as evidenced in the picture of the two of them standing arm in arm on a beach dressed in string bikinis. The other photo showed Rebecca standing proudly alone in the uniform of an army officer. Shira explained tearfully, "I was so proud of her. She worked her way up through the ranks and received her commission to that of lieutenant. The headquarters in Lebanon was her first posting. She was killed a week later." With tears in her eyes she took the album, closed it and held it against her chest for a moment. "It's getting late. We should turn in. Help me with the bed?"

They opened the closet and unfolded the Murphy bed from its place to position it on the floor.

"I'd like to take a shower," said Danielle.

"Me too. You go first."

Danielle took her time in the bathroom, lingering beneath the warm spray of the showerhead. A sudden sense of uncertainty crept into her stomach. She realized she would soon have to face a moment of choice. She went over it a hundred times in her head, rehearsed it like a singer learning a new song. Yet, when it came time to say the words with the warmth of her loving friend next to her in bed, would she be able to follow through? Perhaps she should have said something already…at dinner, or while they sat looking at pictures. Or maybe, if the sensual moments to come proved too powerful to ignore, could it all wait till tomorrow? She just didn't know.

She lay on her back under the flimsy top sheet in T-shirt and panties. Shira entered the room and turned off the light leaving only the glow of the mid-town skyline to peek through half-closed window blinds. She was naked as she eased her way under the sheet, remaining on her side cuddling close to Danielle's form. She put one arm behind Danielle's head and the other reached across trying to maneuver her closer. The younger girl gasped and sat straight up.

The silence of the moment overwhelmed them. Shira relaxed and laid flat on the mattress until she finally asked. "Dani are you okay?"

"Yes," her voice quaked.

"I would never try to make you do anything you didn't want to. You know that, right?"

Danielle bowed her head and dropped down to one elbow. "Shira, I'm so sorry for all the terrible things that happened to you. What those boys did to you, losing Rebecca, all of that. And it would just kill me if we couldn't still be the best of friends and run all around the city and get all goofy. I do love you Shira. But, not in *that* way."

"I understand. I love you as well, yet…" Dani tensed awaiting the caveat. "I don't think I know *how* to be 'goofy.'"

"Don't worry. I'll teach you."

The tense moment passed.

The rest of their weekend was one filled with exploration and wonder. They found the market for fresh vegetables a few blocks south on 2nd Avenue. Shira put a deposit on a twenty-seven inch girl's English Racer at a used bicycle store. It would be hers after a few more payments. They took the subway downtown to Battery Park. A short boat ride brought them to Liberty Island. They giggled on the narrow winding staircase taking them to the top of the Statue of Liberty to take in the breathtaking view of the city from Lady Liberty's crown.

Danielle accompanied Shira to services at a nearby synagogue before dinner at a wonderful Chinese restaurant near the UN Building.

Sunday found the pair of them walking across 42nd Street toward Broadway. Shira marveled at the skyscrapers, theaters and the throngs of people enjoying the weekend in this Mecca of entertainment.

"We should be heading back," Shira announced as the afternoon dwindled toward dusk. "I wanted to make us dinner."

"Nah, we're having too much fun. Besides I have a better idea for dinner."

Her idea turned out to be dirty water hot dogs from a sidewalk stand in front of an office building on Broadway.

"Two please, with the works." Danielle told the hot dog

man. The short, burly vendor hurriedly moved to fill the order.

"Works?" Shira asked with confusion. "What's the works? How do I know I'll like the works?"

"What's not to like? Mustard, sauerkraut, onions and relish."

"Oh my goodness."

Danielle took the first hot dog and gave it to her friend. Shira looked at it with amazement, not quite sure how to approach it. She waited until Danielle got hers. They giggled as she deftly guided one end of the delicacy into her mouth and took a bite. Shira followed her lead, but came away with sauerkraut on her cheek and a clump of relish falling to the sidewalk. Both girls laughed.

"What do you think?" Danielle asked before taking another bite.

"It's really quite tasty." Shira did better her second time.

Danielle finished hers off. "We'll have two more," she told the vendor.

"Sure thing Miss," the man answered.

Shira couldn't believe it. "Danielle? You're going to turn me into a fat cow."

"Don't be silly. We'll work off all the calories on the walk cross-town."

"Is this what you call being goofy?" Shira asked as she gulped down another bite of hot dog.

"*Ab-so-tute-ly.*"

They laughed again. A friendship that began a half a world away was now cemented forever.

Chapter Thirty-Seven:
"The DooWop Shop"

A devastating famine swept through the continent of Africa and specifically the country of Ethiopia, killing nearly one million people. In 1984, producer Bob Geldolf put together a British super group under the name Band Aid to release a record called "Do They Know Its Christmas?" Using the talents of over forty musicians and singers, the song became a worldwide number one hit and raised millions for famine relief.

Noted entertainer and activist Harry Belafonte sought to do the same thing in America. He enlisted the aid of Ken Kragen, an entertainment manager whose client list included Lionel Richie and Kenny Rogers. Soon, Quincy Jones was brought in to produce the tune along with Stevie Wonder and Michael Jackson. The three men set about the task of writing a song named "We Are the World." Wonder, faced with serious time constraints, backed away leaving the other two to complete the international anthem.

The group would perform under the name USA for Africa, an anagram for the organization United Support of Artists for Africa. When word about the project got out, a great number of performers sought to be included. Many were turned away.

Richie and Jackson went into a studio and laid down the music tracks to the song, then duplicated dozens of vocal guides on cassettes. The cassettes were then distributed to the invited guests.

The task of getting such a large number of musically diverse artists together at the same time proved a logistical challenge. A solution was reached by the happy coincidence that many of the participants would be in Los Angeles attending the American Music Awards on the evening of September 28th.

At 9pm, Michael Jackson along with technicians,

engineers and video crews, arrived at the A&M Recording Studios in Hollywood. Many others joined them later, greeted by a makeshift sign which read, "Please check your egos at the door."

The performers took up positions around six microphones set up in a semi-circle. Over the course of the next several hours, Quincy Jones conducted a star studded chorus comprised of artists like Harry Belafonte, Smokey Robinson, Waylon Jennings and Bette Midler. Soloists were chosen, their parts rehearsed and choreographed. Richie and Wonder began the first verse along with Paul Simon, Kenny Rogers, James Ingram, Tina Turner and Billy Joel. They moved into the first chorus with Diana Ross and Michael Jackson. A magically diverse grouping which including Dionne Warwick, Willie Nelson and Al Jerreau sang the second verse. An all-male quartet consisting of Bruce Springsteen, Kenny Loggins, Steve Perry and Daryl Hall belted out the second chorus. The bridge was handled by Michael Jackson again, this time supported by Huey Lewis, Kim Carnes and Cyndi Lauper. Bob Dylan and Ray Charles closed out the final chorus. The session ended at 8am.

The single was released on Thursday, March 7th. Reviews were mixed. One critic called the lyrics "self-aggrandizing." By the following Monday 800,000 copies had been sold. The song went to number one on the *Billboard* chart where it remained for four weeks. "We Are the World" raised millions for the starving people of the planet.

♫ ♫ ♫ ♫ ♫

For the past ten years, Don K. Reed and his *DooWop Shop* was the place to be on the radio dial for the legion of fans that loved the sounds of the fifties and sixties. Every Sunday night Reed, buried in a deep echo effect, worked his magic formula from the WCBS-FM studio on the seventeenth floor of an office building on 52nd Street. For the first three hours of his show he played oldies, traditional songs that were hits on the national charts recorded by highly successful artists. A doo-wop aficionado, he held an abiding love for the more obscure tunes as well. He enjoyed spinning the rarities from the street corner days, the true "one-hit wonders" that hadn't been heard in years. He aired requests and dedications from listeners all over the tri-state area. Reed enjoyed a loyal and fanatical audience.

The show's final hour between 11pm and midnight was reserved for something special. He sent his engineer home and invited guests to join him live in the studio. New York's oldies scene still had many groups looking to break into the music business. If they came to Reed's attention, whether they had a recording contract or not, they were invited to come and sing in what amounted to an on-air audition. New talent had a champion in Don K. Reed.

On one particular night, his guests were doo-wop royalty, the Du-Kanes. After coming out of a commercial break in the final hour, listeners were greeted with a jingle written especially for Reed and his show. Using new lyrics and the melody from "Bouncing a Kiss Off the Moon," the group paid homage to the disc jockey. When the tune finished, Johnny Seracino, Bobby Vitale, Kenny Liebermann and Frankie Mesa applauded, cheered and whistled. Reed seemed humbled.

"Well," Reed began, "it has become something of a tradition here on *The Doowop Shop* for guests to record a little jingle for me. But this one was really special, a tenth anniversary jingle from the Du-Kanes. I wanna welcome you guys to the show." The four men seated around the console in the studio greeted their host.

"Now, I find it hard to believe I've been doing this for ten years, but you guys…you guys have been singing together for what…thirty years?"

"Well, professionally, twenty-seven," Bobby answered, "but Johnny and I started singing together thirty years ago, correct."

"And you, Bobby, along with Johnny and Kenny, are original members?"

"That's right," Johnny said.

"And Frankie, when did you join the group?"

"I joined in sixty-nine. I'm not quite as ancient as these other old farts."

Frankie's comment brought mock moans and laughter from the others.

Reed continued, "And I have to tell you, I'm truly honored because 'Bouncing a Kiss off the Moon,' is one of my favorite songs. But it wasn't your first hit was it?"

"No Don," Johnny answered, "our first big hit was 'When He's Around,' 'Bouncing a Kiss' was our follow-up."

"Two great songs," the disc jockey acknowledged. "I should also tell our listeners we have two other special guests with us here tonight and one of them still seems quite giddy about that jingle we just played."

He referred to that fact that Joseph and Janet sat just a few feet away. They smiled. Janet tried to contain her excitement by covering her mouth with both hands.

"That's right Don," Johnny explained, "that's Joseph and Janet Rabinowitz over there. Janet wrote the new lyrics for the jingle."

"Well then, I think they should both be over here talking with us." The disc jockey motioned for them to come to the microphones. The couple waved him off and shook their heads. Bobby took matters into his own hands. He got up and went into the engineer's area. Grabbing Janet by the hand, he led her across the studio. Joseph followed along. Reed and the rest of the group applauded their arrival. Johnny made room for Janet to have a seat.

"Well, Janet and Joseph *Rabinowitz* is it these days? I remember it as Rabin for a time. Welcome to *The DooWop Shop*."

"Thank you Don," Joseph replied. "Yes that's right,

back to using my full last name Rabinowitz. It's a pleasure to be here."

"And Janet, you wrote the new lyrics? Thank you so much. You certainly had a great reaction to it."

"Yes, when the boys told me they were going to be on the show for your tenth anniversary, I wanted to write something special. It's the first song I've written in many years and as I was sitting over there when I realized that it was going out on the air to millions of listeners, I got a bit overwhelmed I guess."

"Well, who knows, maybe it'll inspire you to write some more great new tunes," Reed suggested.

"Could be," Janet replied with a smile.

The radio host asked a few questions about Chanticleer Enterprises. Reed congratulated Joseph on his renewed success with his concerts, compilation records, tapes and now CDs.

"And, these guys here have a brand new CD out, don't they?" Reed asked.

"Yes, they do and it's selling quite well too. We've redone all their singles and recorded a couple of new cover tunes as well. One in particular, the old Harptones classic, 'That's the Way It Goes,' is making its way up the charts at the present time."

"Well, let's give that one a listen right now."

Reed played the tune and everyone listened to the wonderful lush harmony as it came through the speakers in the studio. The song was highlighted by a strong bass line provided by Frankie Mesa.

"Wow," Reed commented when they came back live. "That was a terrific track."

"You know Don," Joseph sought to wrap up, "they're calling our generation 'baby boomers' these days. But there are also a great many younger people who are discovering just how magical the music of the fifties and sixties can be. Our daughter Danielle will be turning twenty this year. She works with us and it's her job is to sift through all the mail we get from oldies fans, asking if we can find out about some singer or group that's disappeared from the public eye. Then she turns her efforts into finding them to see if they still want to perform. She's quite good at what she does."

"We do love our younger fans," the host agreed. "We've spent a lot of time talking about the music, how about we play some? Let's go all the way back to nineteen fifty-eight and the one that started it all for our guests tonight, the Du-Kanes and 'When He's Around.'"

Chapter Thirty-Eight:
"The Third Rail"

Minutes before the fatal shots were fired, Louis Pizzeria on East Tremont Avenue was crowded with patrons. Just a few doors down the local movie house, the Interboro Theater played host to an oldies show starring the Du-Kanes and three opening acts.

The Seracino family, the Liebermanns and Bobby Vitale were also in the restaurant, adding to the excitement. They sat at a large table in the middle of the room where they garnered much attention. They enjoyed playing shows in their old neighborhood where so many of their friends could come see them. Tickets were hard to come by. Jimmy Stannic was one of the lucky ones.

He sat alone in a booth along the left wall next to the jukebox. He ordered a small pizza and a beer and ate slowly. His attention remained solidly fixed on the table where the performers and their families enjoyed their meal. Not one of them even noticed him, smiled his way or waved hello. It was like he was invisible. His unrequited affection for Barbara had at last twisted all logical thought, *all the years of love I wasted on that cow and still she sits there teasing me. She robbed me of my whole life.*

Occasionally his view became obstructed by someone approaching the jukebox to play records. The owners of the Pizzeria, Louis and Emma Galano, were fans of the group and made sure their hit tunes remained in the restaurant's Wurlitzer record machine. Du-Kanes songs played almost continuously bringing waves and smiles from Johnny and Bobby.

Jimmy's thoughts continued to plague him. *Middle-aged bitches acting like a bunch of friggin teenagers. Why did they treat these guys like they were gods? They weren't any better than he was just because they were famous. He could be famous too, famous like Bobby and Johnny... Famous like David Berkowitz, or the guy who killed John Lennon. All it took was some guts. He had guts. He'd show them all he had guts.*

Jimmy stood and put on the heavy black leather jacket he had folded on the seat next to him. His heart thundered and the blood boiled in his veins. He reached into his jacket pocket and fit his grasp around his .38 caliber revolver as he headed toward the big table.

A female fan had come over to take a snapshot of the group. Kenny, Frankie and Bobby rose and posed on either side of Johnny who remained seated. After the fan was done, Kenny and Frankie walked back to their seats. It was then that Barbara Seracino noticed Jimmy approaching. Her first instinct was to smile until she saw the snarling look on his face. Everything seemed to slow down. Jimmy's hand came out of his jacket pocket holding something – a gun. The horrified look on her face caused both Bobby and Johnny to turn around.

By the time they focused on Jimmy, his arm was raised and the gun aimed squarely at Johnny's chest. Barbara managed to scream out her husband's name. For some reason Bobby lunged forward putting his own body directly into the line of fire.

The .38 barked twice startling everyone in the restaurant. Both bullets hit Bobby in the middle of his chest sending him flailing backward into Johnny. The men went sprawling to the floor. Patrons screamed. Someone yelled, "Call the police!" Another shouted, "Somebody call an ambulance!" Several people rushed toward the back of the restaurant in an effort to help.

Jimmy bolted to the front entrance knocking down anyone foolish enough to try to stop him. Two young men followed him out the door, but did not pursue further.

Johnny maneuvered Bobby's body and propped him up against his chest. He stared down at his gravely wounded friend. Barbara stood behind him clutching him tightly as she cried aloud. Kenny and Frankie tried to keep everyone else away. Bobby's eyes were open, his gaze fixed and confused, showing no indication that he felt any pain. He tried to say something but simply coughed.

"Don't try to talk man," Johnny's voice cracked, "help is on the way."

"Johnny... I love you man." Bobby's eyes bulged for a second, his body stiffened and his head turned slowly into his best friend's chest.

Bobby Vitale was gone.

Within minutes of the shooting, uniformed officers from the 45th Precinct were on the scene talking to witnesses. One of the young boys who followed the shooter outside told them he took off running toward the corner of Tremont Avenue and Bruckner Boulevard. There, the BX 40 bus line ran east to Throggs Neck and west to the Westchester Square Subway station.

At the corner candy store, a frightened woman gave them more information. "Some guy in a black leather jacket came running down the street like a maniac. He jumped on a bus heading to the Square."

The police believed their suspect was trying to get to the subway. They used their hand radios to notify cops at Westchester Square of the details of their pursuit. Those officers were disappointed by the news they got from the token booth clerk on duty at the station.

"Yeah, some guy flashed his Transit ID card and jumped the turnstile. Employees ain't supposed to do that, but this guy was in a real rush."

"Did he make the train?" one cop asked.

"Think so. Downtown express just pulled out."

Two detectives, one black and the other white, joined the hunt. Beat cops kept the salt and pepper team updated. Together they formulated a plan of action.

"Is there a Transit Cop on that train?" the white detective asked.

A uniformed officer answered, "We're trying to find that out now."

"We can have the transit people radio the engineer and stop the train," the black detective offered.

"No. Not yet," his partner replied. "If our guy panics and takes hostages we'll have a whole shit storm to deal with." Still trying to come up with something he asked another question, "The train goes underground at Hunt's Point, right?"

The token clerk nodded, "that's right."

"What are the stops right after that?"

"Longwood Avenue, East One-hundred Forty-ninth Street and then One Forty-third after that."

After some quick calculations, the white detective had an idea. "Six blocks, that's pretty well contained. Radio your dispatcher to stop the train midway between One Forty-ninth and One Forty-third."

His partner offered, "But if he works for the transit authority, he probably knows his way around pretty good in those tunnels."

"Yeah, still, I'd rather have him cooped up underground than on the loose somewhere outside."

♫ ♫ ♫ ♫ ♫

Jimmy Stannic did indeed know his way around the subway tunnels. When the train he was on came to a sudden halt between stations, he knew he had to take action. Since he had no desire to take a hostage and hurt anyone else, his only choice was to leave the train.

He made his way between two cars, slipped under the connecting hardware and jumped into the darkness. There would be a ladder to an emergency exit just a short distance ahead. If he could make it to the ladder he could extend the chase. The longer he remained on the run, the bigger the headlines would be. Back in the restaurant he saw both

Johnny and Bobby fall. Did he kill them both? It really didn't matter; killing two celebrities would only add to his fame.

He'd gone along the darkened tunnel about one hundred yards when he heard shouting voices closing in behind him. Then he saw the beams of several flashlights crisscrossing in the tunnel ahead. He was cut off. No chance to make it to the emergency exit. Jimmy put his hand in his pocket and felt for the revolver. He didn't want to get into a shoot-out with the cops.

One of the flashlight beams shone in his face, blinding him, forcing him to raise his hand and shield his eyes.

"Freeze right there!" A voice called out echoing throughout the tunnel. "Drop the weapon!"

He complied and raised his hands above his head in surrender. The cops came running toward him. Jimmy thought of David Berkowitz and how frail, frightened and fragile he looked after his capture. The power he spoke of that night in Li'l Abners was gone. Now, he was just a common criminal judged to be insane, destined to rot away in a prison cell.

Jimmy didn't want that happening to him.

The first police officer to reach him was young, and in his twenties. He pointed a flashlight at Jimmy with one hand and his service revolver with the other. The cop appeared calm and ready to do his duty.

Jimmy smiled at him, threw out his chest and in an act of deliberate defiance, slid his foot a few inches until it came in contact with the third rail. A low, barely audible hum accompanied the high voltage electric charge that coursed through his body, searing his organs, killing him instantly. His smoldering corpse fell over onto the tracks. The young police officer vomited.

Jimmy Stannic never got his front-page headlines, but his deed did make the papers, a small two-column story on page four of the *Post* and page three in the *Daily News*. Both stories featured the picture the fan took of the group in the restaurant and focused on Bobby and the group, but it did describe his killer as being, "...a mentally ill neighborhood man many people called Geep."

🎵🎵🎵🎵🎵

Bobby's funeral Mass at Our Lady of Solace Church was attended by hundreds of fans and people from the music world. Bobby's sister Diane was there with her husband. But it was left to Johnny to embrace and console her as they sat in the first pew during the service. Johnny delivered a tearful, touching eulogy of loss and friendship calling Bobby more like a brother than a friend. Joseph spoke of the singer's talent and the joy he brought to millions of fans. As everyone left the church, Joseph noticed Althea and Evie Rhodes seated in a back row.

Bobby was buried next to his mother in St. Raymond's Cemetery in a plot the singer purchased in his more successful times. No fans were permitted at the gravesite. Joseph, Janet and Danielle were invited back to the Seracino house for coffee but begged off. He recognized the need for the remaining members of the group to have their private time to grieve.

A singing group as closely knit as the Du-Kanes shared a solemn bond both in their on stage persona and in their private time. Johnny, Kenny and Frankie would sit alone, raise a glass to a fallen comrade, alternately laugh and cry over shared memories and in the end...harmonize.

Chapter Thirty-Nine:
"Regents Bank of G.B."

Chanticleer Enterprises occupied a suite of offices in a three-story building on Purchase Street in Rye. A matronly woman in her fifties, named Lois Schenck, managed a full-time staff of five. Handpicked by Leo Klein, she had been his New York assistant back when the new company formed. Now with Leo gone, she was in charge of the day-to-day operations with regard to scheduling the concerts, dealing with the venues, travel and accommodations for the artists. She was also the company's accountant. While she always dressed in business attire, the others, Karlin the receptionist, Alan and Connie, who handled requests for tickets, and Danielle remained quite casual.

Danielle worked at her desk in a large office she shared with Joseph. Today she worked alone. Karlin, the pretty dark haired Puerto Rican receptionist, popped her head in the doorway.

"There's a call for you on line two. He says his name is TJ Russell."

Danielle looked up in a flash. "Who?"

"TJ Russell?" She repeated and shrugged not yet recognizing any significance.

Danielle picked up the receiver, but hesitated before pressing the plastic button that would connect the call. "Hello?"

"Is this Danielle?"

"Yes?"

"This is TJ Russell. Listen, I know you're gonna think this is crazy, but I need to see you. Can you meet me?"

"Um...meet you? Meet you when?"

"Now. I'm here in Rye, at the train station. I wouldn't blame you if you told me to fuck off, but I'm in trouble. It's about my record company."

She sensed the urgency in his voice and her curiosity

got the better of her. "There's a café just across the street called The Depot. Do you see it?"

"I'll find it."

"I can be there in five minutes." She hung up the phone and grabbed her pocket book from a desk drawer. Suddenly, Karlin was again in the doorway.

"Hey, was that *the* TJ Russell?"

Danielle had no time for her. "I'm going to lunch," she said before heading toward the door.

♫♫♫♫♫

TJ was already seated at a table in the back of the café when Danielle arrived. He thanked her for coming and they both ordered coffee. After being served, the singer began to explain his dilemma. He wasn't long into his narrative when Danielle interrupted, "I think you should really be telling all this to my father."

"The last time your dad and I talked face to face it didn't go so good," TJ reminded her.

"Let me call him. I'm sure he'll meet with you."

She called home, using the public telephone on the wall inside the café's entrance. She returned a moment later. "C'mon he's waiting for us."

♫♫♫♫♫

They arrived at the house to find Joseph and Janet seated on the sectional couch in their living room. TJ was appropriately hesitant, nervous and even embarrassed about being there. His attitude and prior encounters with the three of them had all been somewhat combative. Yet here they were, seemingly receptive to hearing him out. Joseph stood to shake his hand as he entered.

"Mr. Rabinowitz, thank you so much for seeing me," he said with sincerity.

"You've met my wife I believe?"

He nodded her way. "Ma'am."

Janet nodded, but did not respond.

Joseph motioned for TJ to have a seat. Danielle made herself comfortable on an easy chair off in one corner. "He's got some bad problems with Alexis Records."

"Richie Conforti and his bunch," Janet offered. "We've had our own run-ins with that crowd."

"Why don't you tell me all about it?" Joseph added.

"It has to do with my royalties. My records are selling like crazy, always have been. My concerts are sold out. But, I've never been able to get an accurate accounting of what I'm supposed to be getting. Now, don't get me wrong, I've always been taken care of, expenses, clothes, a condo in Greenwich Village…and anytime I've needed cash Mr. Conforti would always cut me a check…sometimes for as much as two or three thousand dollars at a time."

"Have you spoken to them about it?" Joseph asked.

"Yessir, many times. But they just say that the company has expenses too, studio time, pressing the records, publicity and such. And they say that has to be paid out before I can have my money. I understand all that. Still, it don't seem right to me. About a year ago, I started pushing the issue pretty hard and that's when Mr. Conforti called me into his office for a meeting," the young man paused, seeming reluctant to continue.

"TJ, you came to me for help. I can't do that unless I know everything. What happened at that meeting?"

♫ ♫ ♫ ♫ ♫

Richie Conforti's office was lavish and well furnished. He sat in a high back bronze colored leather chair behind a huge mahogany desk. Gold records adorned the walls all around the office perimeter. There were no visitor's chairs on the opposite side of the desk. The only other seating was a leather sofa pushed against the far wall. It was Richie's way of keeping total control of the dealings in his office. He liked to keep people at a distance and make them shout across the room.

For this particular meeting, TJ sat on one end of the sofa with Phil Gambetta at the other end to provide an added bit of security. Richie held court for the first fifteen minutes or so, complimenting the young singer on his great ability as a performer and just how much he meant to the company. Finally, he came around to his point.

"You wanna know who gets the bulk of your hard earned cash kid? Uncle Sam, that's who. Taxes… the government kills us all with taxes."

Phil voiced his opinion, "Fucking feds would tax us every time we took a shit if they thought they could get away with it."

"Phillie is exaggerating of course, though not by much. You see, if you were a construction worker or a truck driver you'd belong to a labor union. They would deduct a portion of your pay for benefits like a medical plan in the event you got sick, or a pension plan to put aside money for you when you retired. Sadly, as a performer, you don't have any such luxuries. That's why it's important to be smart with your money." Richie opened one of his desk drawers and produced a stack of papers he then placed on the desk. "I consider myself to be a smart man. We are prepared to offer you a wonderful opportunity to join us in protecting your hard earned money." Phil Gambetta stood and walked across the plush carpeting to the desk. He picked up the papers and returned to the couch. He handed the papers to TJ as Richie continued, "By signing those papers you give us the authority to invest a percentage of your royalties in an off-shore bank in the Bahamas. Uncle Sam will know nothing about it and can't touch a nickel. Think of it as a shelter for your earnings."

"It sounds interesting. I'd like to look this over," TJ said.

"Sure. Go ahead. Take your time," Richie replied.

"You...you want me to sign it right here...right now?"

"Whattsamatter kid...doncha trust us?" The accusing tone in Phil's voice sent a chill up TJ's spine.

Richie broke the tension of the moment. "It's also important that you understand that unfortunately we're not able to offer this option to all our artists. You are the shining star in our galaxy...very special. It's imperative that what we do here be kept in the strictest confidence."

"Do like Richie tells you kid. Be smart. Sign the papers."

♪♪♪♪♪

"Do you remember the name of the bank?" Joseph asked.

TJ nodded. "The Regents Bank of Grand Bahama. And the reason I remember it is because last week the bank folded...closed up shop. Conforti called me in the other day and told me he was sorry... everyone lost their money."

"Omigod," Danielle uttered.

"That's awful," Janet said. "You lost everything?"

TJ nodded as he continued, "The thing of it is, *they* didn't seem all that upset over it."

"That doesn't surprise me. Those guys are a couple of slippery characters." Joseph thought for a moment. "How did you leave off with them?"

"They told me to take some time off. I'm supposed to start rehearsals in two weeks for a big show at Madison Square Garden."

"Good, because I want you to stay here in the house with us overnight. Then tomorrow, I want you to repeat everything you just told us to our attorney."

TJ stood and became quite animated. "No man, I can't do that."

Joseph tried to reason with the young man. "It's like

my wife said earlier. We've had dealings with these people before. They can be very dangerous. Tax evasion is a serious crime. If you don't get out from underneath this now, it might not be possible later."

"You've got nothing to lose by listening to our lawyer," Janet offered. "She can advise you and then you can decide on what to do."

TJ looked across the room at Danielle who nodded and smiled.

Though the guest bedroom was quite comfortable, TJ couldn't sleep. His conscience bothered him. At about 1am he got out of bed, dressed and tried to walk downstairs as quietly as possible. As he headed toward the door he spotted a light on in the kitchen. He wandered in that direction and was surprised to find Danielle seated at the counter, dressed in gym shorts and a halter-top drinking a glass of milk.

"Leaving without saying goodbye?" she asked.

"Something like that."

"Milk?"

"No, I'm good." Faced with the need to explain himself he began, "I don't want you to think I'm ungrateful or anything, but I was lying up there thinking about how sorry I was for dragging you and your family into all this. It's my mess. I should be the one to clear it up."

"So why did you then…drag us into it?"

"I don't know. Maybe it's because your father is the only really honorable person I know."

Danielle drank the last gulp of her milk, stood and brought her glass to the sink. She faced him and asked, "Then why don't you take his advice and talk to the lawyer?"

As he sought an answer, he felt a twinge of embarrassment. He suddenly realized he never really took the time to notice just how pretty she was. Her looks, fiery character, and steadfast loyalty to the things she held dear combined to form a unique personality.

Tired of waiting for his answer, Danielle pushed away from the counter, headed toward the door and then hesitated. "Just turn off the light when you go back upstairs."

Not long after she left the room, he did just that.

Chapter Forty:
"Out Of a Clear Blue Sky"

By the time Marlene-Klein Sussman finished taking TJ's statement, she had nine pages of Gregg style steno notes on a legal sized yellow pad.

"What do you think?" Joseph asked her.

Marlene replied, "Well, I'd like to make a few discreet telephone inquiries…see what I can come up with on this Regents Bank. That might give us a better idea of what we're dealing with."

"Fine. You can use the phone in my den."

As they moved off Janet suggested, "Why don't I make us all some lunch?"

That left Danielle and TJ alone in the living room.

"You okay?" Danielle asked him.

"I could use a cigarette. I don't suppose…"

"Not in this house. There's a grocery store a few blocks away. The walk might do us both good."

"Yeah, lets do that."

On their way to the store TJ remarked, "It sure is a lot more peaceful up here than it is in the city. I'd never be able to walk around the Village without drawin a crowd and havin a bunch of fans pestering for an autograph, or tryin to take a picture."

"You don't seem to think very much of your fans, do you?"

Her blunt question brought about a nervous chuckle. "Well, I wouldn't put it quite *that way*."

"It's just that you don't seem comfortable with all the attention. I mean, that's what you get for being such a big star…a celebrity," Danielle told him.

"I suppose you could be right. There was a time when I used to think that that's all I ever wanted…to be famous, have my name in lights…party all the time. Now, with all this bullshit that's going on around me, I feel like this being a star isn't all it's cracked up to be."

"Don't worry, my dad will figure something out."

As they entered the grocery store, they passed two young girls on their way out. One of them did a double take when she looked at TJ. Deciding she was wrong about seeing a rock and roll star in her neighborhood grocery store, she and her friend continued on.

The exchange made TJ antsy.

Danielle giggled. "Maybe it's *not* as different up here as you thought. Don't sweat it. We'll take the long way home along the shoreline. No one will recognize you there."

The walk home took them along the tree-lined approach to Playland. This late in the season, the amusement park was closed. Pedestrians often made their way along the quiet paths outside the gates bordering the parking areas.

She led him to one of her favorite places, a stand of willow trees located on a grassy knoll tucked back from the road. The trees stood some thirty-plus feet in height. Rounded open crowns of sweeping leaves created a canopy that was truly dramatic. TJ was impressed.

"This is almost like back home," he said.

"Isn't it beautiful?" Danielle asked. She plopped down to the ground bracing herself with the palms of her hands. "I've been a city girl all my life so this is a real treat for me. I come here a lot just to daydream."

TJ sat down next to her, bent his knees and leaned forward to rest his arms on them. "What is it you dream about?"

"I've been pretty lucky really. I have a great family. I love working for my dad, and I get the chance to meet people who have made some really great music. Joseph says next year, when I turn twenty-one, he'll let me run some of the tours to different parts of the country."

"What about your personal life...having a family of your own?"

"You mean like a boyfriend and stuff like that? My

knight in shining armor?" Danielle laughed. "My mother used to tell me about how, when she was young, she used to dream about her knight in shining armor...how he'd come along, sweep her up and carry her off to live happily ever after. And then one day there was a knock on the door and there he was...out of a clear blue sky." Her eyes brightened and her smile made dimples on the sides of her mouth. "They had some hard times. Heck, if it wasn't for the hard times I wouldn't be sitting here talking to you."

TJ looked deeply into her eyes, fell back on one elbow, leaned in and kissed her...out of a clear blue sky.

♫♫♫♫♫

When they got back to the house they found Janet had made sandwiches and salad. They ate quietly. After lunch everyone gathered in the living room once again. Marlene had news.

"It appears the IRS has been looking into this Regents Bank for quite some time. A contact I have told me that they've been involved in covert operations with the CIA dating back to the Cuban Missile Crisis. I was also able to find out that Alexis Records had no accounts with the bank."

"How is that possible?" TJ asked anxiously. "I *know* I saw that name on those papers."

"I don't doubt you," Marlene said. "While the record company had no accounts, Richie Conforti and Phil Gambetta did, personal accounts with balances in the millions of dollars."

"And yet TJ says they didn't bat an eye when they told him the money was lost," Joseph commented.

Marlene explained further, "That's because they *didn't* lose their money. They closed their accounts two days *before* the bank went under. That means they had some insider trading information which makes this whole mess even more illegal." Now there was silence with stunned looks all around.

Marlene looked to TJ. "There was no account in your name either. You must have unknowingly given them power of attorney to act on your behalf."

"So am I in the clear?" TJ asked.

"No," Marlene answered quickly. "The IRS is going to be all over this. When they get to the bottom of it, you can still be implicated in a tax avoidance scheme. Which gives me more cause for concern."

"How so Marlene?" Janet asked.

"The Viola branch of the crime syndicate has come under investigation many times in the past, going all the way back to the payola days. They always seem to come out of it unscathed. For them to be involved in something as flimsy as this tax shelter scheme just seems so sloppy."

"Do you think perhaps the two of them are skimming from the Violas?"

The inference was almost too impossible to consider. Marlene thought carefully before responding. "I think that *is* possible. If that's the case and the mob believes that TJ is involved. He could be in grave danger."

"What do you think he should do?" Janet asked.

"I think it would be in his best interest to come forward to the authorities. There's a new prosecutor in the US Attorney's office. His name is Giuliani. He's been making a name for himself prosecuting members of organized crime under the RICO act."

"What's a RICO act?" Danielle wanted to know.

"The Racketeer Influenced and Corrupt Organization Act. It gives prosecutors added powers to seize assets and property if it's believed they've been attained by illegal means. It's proven very successful."

Janet asked a question, "What will happen if he does go to the authorities?"

"It's possible he could be granted immunity."

Everyone looked at TJ.

"I'll do whatever it takes," the singer said.

"Good," Marlene concluded. "Until we can get things going, he needs to be kept under wraps."

"I think he should stay here." All eyes fell upon Danielle. "Why not? It's the last place anybody would think to look for him."

"She could be right," Joseph offered.

"Hold on a second," TJ complained, "I just can't camp out someplace. I need some of my things. I gotta go back to my place."

"I'll go with you," Danielle was quick to say.

"No!" Marlene was emphatic in her response. She spoke directly to Joseph, "I can't impress on you the absolute need for you and your family to keep out of this." Unless there's someone you can trust implicitly, he'll have to go alone."

Danielle had the answer. "I know just the person."

Shira Bar-On was more than agreeable to help without asking very many questions. She arranged for a car and driver from the Council where she worked to meet TJ at a prearranged time outside his apartment building. Shira would remain with him until he packed some of his things and was ready to return to Rye.

While TJ was gone, Marlene had other things to convey to Joseph.

"Before long, this is all going to be way beyond my expertise. Russell is going to need a top criminal attorney. I can recommend one."

"Fine," Joseph said.

"The other thing is...he needs to understand that once he's made his deal with the US Attorney, if there are indictments...a trial...he'll be called to testify. If they are convicted, those gangsters are going to jail. TJ will be a hunted man."

"The government can protect him, right?" Janet asked.

Marlene nodded. "They'll put him in the Federal

Witness Protection Program. He'll be re-located with a new identity. But likely as not, he'll never be able to perform in public again."

The news hit them all hard.

"Oh God no," Janet said.

"Daddy you can't let that happen," Danielle argued, "I won't let it happen. I'll tell him not to testify."

"Dani," Joseph tried to reason with her. "We shouldn't go jumping to conclusions. Marlene is just giving us options."

"I mean it, I swear...I'll tell him so." Danielle stormed out of the room.

"Danielle, come back here," Janet called after her.

"Let her go," Joseph advised.

Marlene gathered her things to leave. "It's not *an* option Joseph, it's the *only* option. If Russell wants to stay out of jail, or worse if the Viola's get to him, he needs to understand these things. Call me after he decides what he wants to do."

After Marlene left the house, Joseph crossed the room. Janet had moved to the large picture window overlooking their backyard. There Danielle sat cross-legged on the diving board of their pool. Her shoulders shook. She was crying. Joseph stood close as his wife nestled back into him.

Janet whispered. "Remember when we first moved in here and that terrible animal was pilfering our trash in the middle of the night?"

"Rocky Racoon?" he replied. Danielle named the nocturnal invader after the song from the Beatles White Album. "How could I forget? Dani wanted to adopt it."

"And we had all to do – to convince her that raccoons could not be domesticated...that she could not have it as a pet. And that if Rocky bit her, she would have to endure a long painful series of rabies shots."

"Luckily the Animal Control people solved that problem."

"I don't think the Animal Control people can help us this time."

"You figure Dani wants to adopt TJ?"

"Something like that…or worse. What do you figure their difference in ages is?"

"Eight…nine years maybe."

"Joseph she's way too young…"

Her husband interrupted her, "Shhh…shhh. She's a big girl…she knows what she's doing. This situation is gonna change TJ's life immensely. She's just being a comfort to him now."

As Danielle sat sobbing, she replayed the earlier events with TJ under the willow tree over and over in her mind. His first kiss was unexpected to be sure. She welcomed it and all that followed.

Against all logic, she was in love with him.

♫ ♫ ♫ ♫ ♫

When TJ got back to the house Joseph spoke to him about the repercussions he faced by testifying in any criminal action. His kneejerk reaction was about as one would expect, the boy flew off the handle.

"No, man there's got to be some other way!" He screamed, paced and shook his head. "I shoulda kept my mouth shut bout all this. I might as well be dead than give up my singing."

Joseph tried to reason with him. "You've come to a place where your career has to take a back seat to your freedom…your safety for Chrissake."

It took some time for the young man to absorb the magnitude of the decision he was now forced to make. Joseph realized he needed some space to be alone.

"C'mon Danielle, TJ has some thinking to do."

Joseph went upstairs and Danielle made her way toward the patio doors.

For a long moment TJ just sat there covering his face with his hands until he sensed he was not alone. He looked to see that Danielle had come back into the house.

"Why don't you just tell them all to go screw themselves and take your chances." Danielle's whispered advice, while sincere, didn't present a sensible resolution to the matter and TJ knew it.

"No, your dad and his lawyer are right," he finally relented. "We've gone over this from every angle. Conforti's got papers with my signature on them putting me right in the middle of this thing. I could go to jail or worse. If those guys *are* skimming off the mob, I could end up with a bullet in my head. I got no choice."

Danielle crossed the room and reached down to take his hand. He stood and followed her out of the house.

♪♪♪♪♪

The next day, Joseph telephoned Marlene and informed her of TJ's decision to cooperate. She then recommended TJ hire Bruce Mulligan, a prominent defense attorney to act as his legal counsel. After agreeing to take the case, Mulligan set up a meeting with the US Attorney's office, informing them that he had a "star witness" willing to testify against the Violas. This pleased Giuliani very much. In return, Mulligan was able to tell TJ that if his testimony resulted in the conviction of the mobsters, he would be granted full immunity. The singer agreed to these terms with one condition.

"I want to play that concert I have scheduled at the Garden. This ain't negotiable."

Mulligan knew Giuliani was not a man known for his patience and would soon be pressing him for the identity of his star witness. Mulligan gave in to TJ's demand and a written deal was worked out.

Until the concert, TJ would remain ensconced in the Rabinowitz home.

Chapter Forty-One:
"Rudy"

Rudolph Giuliani, the son of two Italian immigrants, was born in East Flatbush, New York. As a child, he saw his father Harold convicted of felony assault and robbery and sentenced to a term in Sing Sing Prison. Upon his release, his father became involved in an organized crime family serving as enforcer for his brother-in-law.

Rudy, as he came to be known, somehow managed to avoid any involvement in criminal activity. He attended parochial elementary and high school where he excelled academically. Giuliani majored in political science at Manhattan College and went on to NYU Law where he made *Law Review*. Perhaps to purge his family name of its past criminal involvement, he went to work as a federal prosecutor in the Justice Department as an Associate Attorney General.

Like Ronald Reagan before him, Rudy switched his political party affiliation from Democrat to Republican. Because of his desire to litigate cases against corruption and organized crime, he accepted a demotion with his appointment as US Attorney for the Southern District of New York. Using the broad parameters of the RICO statute, he conducted the Mafia Commission Trial winning indictments on nearly a dozen of New York City's organized crime figures. As Giuliani himself put it, "Our approach...is to wipe out the five families."

One high-level crime boss was said to comment, "That guy Giuliani has got his eye on City Hall. He wants to be mayor." Another gave him an even greater accolade. "Shit, if he gets these convictions, the motherfucker could run for president."

♫♫♫♫♫

They were naked in the queen size bed in Danielle's

bedroom. TJ lay on his back and Danielle rested her head on his chest. Their legs intertwined.

Danielle expected TJ to be an angry lover, owing to the combative nature he exhibited in his everyday behavior. Happily, she found out otherwise. Whatever *she* lacked in experience *he* made up for in a rock star way. Yet, as though being truly cognizant of her age, he was tender and gentle. The sun had not yet risen, but it would soon be time for TJ to leave.

"Our timing really sucks," he whispered.

"Quiet you. I'm trying not to think about it," she said without looking at him.

"We have to face facts. After this show at the Garden, I'm going to surrender myself to the US Marshals. They'll babysit me until the trial, which could be months away. After that, who knows where they'll send me? I don't guess we'll see each other after that." He spoke softly and tenderly as he turned to take her in his arms.

Danielle pulled away and sat up. "We'll find a way. Shira will help us. She knows all about how to do this secret stuff."

"And put you and your folks at risk? No, Dani I could never do that."

"I don't care about the risk. I love you and I want to be with you. I'll go wherever they send you." Danielle was near tears.

"That's crazy talk." TJ left the bed and got dressed. Danielle rose and went to the bathroom, when she returned she was wearing a robe.

"I'm not giving up on this," she warned him.

TJ said nothing. He just smiled and held her hand as they left the pool house. As they'd done before, they strolled together across the short distance to the patio doors at the back of the house. There, TJ would enter and sneak his way upstairs to the guest bedroom.

This time proved to be different. They were taken

aback when they saw Janet sitting in a patio chair waiting. She had a stern look on her face. The couple stood frozen. Danielle put her hand to her face to shield her embarrassment. TJ was barely able to speak.

"Mrs. Rabinowitz…I…"

"I'd like a word with my daughter if you don't mind," Janet said flatly.

TJ looked at Danielle who told him, "Go ahead upstairs."

As TJ moved into the house, Danielle averted her mother's gaze and wrapped the robe more tightly around her otherwise naked body.

"How long has this been going on?" her mother asked sternly.

"A week or so…I don't know. What difference does it make?"

"It certainly makes a difference Dani, I…"

"I'm really in no mood for a lecture Mother."

Stolen moments of intimacy was not a new concept to Janet. When she was only sixteen, she and Joseph were guilty of the same thing, both in Cleveland, at her father's home and then again at Joseph's parent's apartment in New York. Yet, she somehow reconciled the difference in the situations in that she and Joseph intended to be married and share a life together. "I don't want to lecture you. I'm merely pointing out that you're making a big mistake. In a few days this boy will be gone and you won't ever see him again."

"I *will* see him again!" Danielle said angrily. "I told him I'd go anywhere with him…I love him."

"That's crazy. How can you love him? You hardly know him."

"Why is that so crazy? You told me you fell in love with Joseph without ever having met him just from seeing his picture. And Dad told me he fell in love with *you* just from reading the poems you sent to your brother."

There was no arguing with her logic, yet her mother

tried. "Think of what you are saying. If you go away with him you won't be able to have any contact with any of us. You'll be giving up your family…your whole life."

Before her mother could say anymore Danielle quietly said, "Yeah, that's right. It is my life…my decision."

She walked away leaving her mother to absorb her answer.

Chapter Forty-Two:
"Move It On Over"

Rumors circulating around the New York music scene brought about a buzz of excitement with regard to the upcoming TJ Russell concert at Madison Square Garden. Members of his regular backup band spoke of an entire revamping of the material. They claimed they were only rehearsing for half a show. This led many to speculate that Russell planned to do the second half all acoustic, with only him and a guitar onstage. This angered many of TJ's fans, who looked upon it much in the same way Bob Dylan's fans reacted when that normally acoustic singer went electric decades earlier.

Russell added to the mystery by his disappearance each night, after rehearsal, in a long black town car that picked him up and whisked him away. Paparazzi standing vigil at his condo confirmed that no such vehicle ever dropped him off at that location. It became apparent that whatever surprises TJ had planned for his audience, it would have to wait until the night of his sold out performance.

♫♫♫♫♫

Ten tickets to a luxury box on the periphery of the top level were sent as a gift to the American Jewish Council in the name of Miriam Salberg. Ms. Salberg would use six of the tickets for herself, her two daughters and three of their friends. The four remaining tickets she gave to her special assistant at the Council, Shira Bar-On, who in turn invited the three closest friends she had in America, the Rabinowitz family. In that way, no one would know they were even at the show and the connection between the family and Russell remained a secret.

♫♫♫♫♫

The houselights dimmed fashionably late at eight twenty leading to the first surprise of the evening. There was no opening act.

TJ Russell captivated his audience with the very first chords that rang forth from the massive speakers on stage. He sang with confidence and enthusiasm for a solid hour, belting out his many hits and songs from his new LP due out in the near future. A short intermission followed. The crowd sensed something special was in the air when a group of roadies moved to reset the stage for the second half of the show. They rolled out a Hammond B-3 organ and accompanying speaker cabinet, equipment not standard for TJ's solo act.

TJ appeared alone and walked to the microphone center stage. "You may recognize these next guys." He turned and extended his hand to the wings. The crowd went wild when Cam Pierson came out followed by the remaining members of Amadeus.

In the time since he abandoned the group, TJ had adamantly refused to perform any of his former band's material. That obviously would not be the case on this night.

The long set that followed had TJ out front on all the hits he had with the band. Then he relinquished the lead microphone to Cam Pierson who continued on with the chart hits Amadeus had since Russell's departure.

The response to this unannounced reunion was deafening. TJ returned to center stage and played the tenacious opening guitar strains of "Sweet Home Alabama." The extended performance thrilled everyone in the arena. After the song, the musicians lined up to accept the adulation and applause of the crowd. It would have been a fitting end to a fabulous show, but when Pierson and the others returned to their instruments it became apparent they weren't done yet.

"And here's a little something my daddy did."

With that short introduction TJ counted off an intro to "Move it On Over," the signature song that launched Teddy

Boyette to stardom.

Emotions ran high throughout the building but none higher than in the luxury suite high above where Joseph, Janet and Danielle sat with tears in their eyes. They watched as TJ swung his guitar over his shoulder and onto his back freeing his hands. He exhorted the crowd to sing along with him. He removed the microphone from its stand and after singing each line of the chorus. He extended the microphone out across the edge of the stage and let the crowd answer back in a choir of thousands of voices.

After the ovation that followed, Cam played a chilling B-3 introduction and keyboard riff in a new arrangement of another Boyette classic, "Within A Wooded Chapel." The B-3 growled out a long organ riff that rang out to the rafters. This was the showstopper, a reverent rendition that created a cathedral-like atmosphere and provided the emotional exclamation point the evening deserved.

The performers stood together embracing and waving to the throng. The members of Amadeus peeled back to leave TJ alone to enjoy the adulation of his fans. The crowd cheered long after the houselights came up.

At the backstage celebration afterwards, Russell was most conspicuous in his absence. Reporters were left to interview Cam Pierson.

"Cam," one reporter called out, "can you tell us how all this came about?"

"It was as big a surprise to us as it was to you. The guy called me out of nowhere and said he wanted us to come out and do his show with him. After all the bullshit he put us through, I figured he must have an inoperable brain tumor or something. It took some convincing, but I think it came out okay."

A female reporter stuck a cassette recorder in his face. "Can we expect more reunion shows like this?"

Pierson simply shrugged. "I got no idea. I guess you

gotta ask him."

"Where is he?" the reporter asked.

"Yeah man, where'd he go?" asked another.

"Fucked if I know," Cam answered. "Some old guy grabbed him up the minute he came off stage. But I wouldn't worry. TJ has never been the shy type. He'll show up shooting his mouth off sooner or later."

Chapter Forty-Three:
"A Flock of Seagulls"

In the end, loyalty was the only real mistake Max Seiderman made. Perhaps he truly believed that if he remained loyal to the family he could avoid the wrath of Carlo Viola now that the criminal empire was about to come under intense scrutiny.

So, when summoned, he went without question to a meeting with Carlo at an after hour's club the mob owned in Brooklyn. The place was deserted except for Carlo and several of his bodyguards.

Max sat across from his boss who was irate. "My guy in the DA's office tells me Giuliani has a witness stashed away someplace. A witness from the fucking record company!" His anger accelerating with every word, he was out of his chair and in the old man's face in a shot. "That was your gig you fucking Jew! The old man put you in charge of that a long time ago!"

"It wasn't me Carlo, I swear. It was Conforti and Gambetta. They done all of it. That bank in the Bahamas...all that fucking money they skimmed. I didn't know nothin about any of that, I swear."

"There's not a hole deep enough anywhere in the world where those two cocksuckers can hide for very long," Carlo vowed. "But it ain't them I'm worried about Max."

"You don't need to worry about anything Carlo. I went through the record company's office myself. I burned or shredded every piece of paper that could lead back to the family. There's no paper trail."

Carlo wasn't re-assured. "I don't give a shit about any paper trail either."

Max felt a sudden rush of fear. "You can't mean to say you're worried about me? I been loyal to you and your old man for over fifty fucking years. I wouldn't ever say anything to anybody."

♫♫♫♫♫

The last group of trucks made the wide turn onto Brush Avenue waiting their turn through the high chain-link fence leading into the Ferry Point Park Landfill in the Bronx. The 243-acre area was designated as the place to compact and bury raw garbage and construction debris. Every day, dozens of City Sanitation vehicles and private dump trucks made their way up the man-made mountain of waste material to the tipping area where they would dispose of their payload.

A green truck from the Potenzo Sanitation Company would be the last to unload on this day. The driver backed his vehicle slowly up the steep incline before leveling off on the thick plateau of garbage. He engaged the switch that lifted the body of the dump truck upward from the chassis. Hundreds of pounds of raw garbage spewed forth. The driver inched the truck forward to allow the rest of his payload to be distributed evenly across the plateau. Among the uneaten or discarded food from a dozen or more restaurants along his route, were three large black plastic garbage bags. They contained the dismembered body parts of three men sprinkled with lye to hasten decomposition. Richie Conforti and Phil Gambetta met a traitor's fate. Max Seiderman failed in his duties to properly administer the operations assigned to him and became a liability.

As dusk approached a temporary quiet fell over the landfill. You heard them before you saw them, the squealing din of thousands of seagulls flocking westward en masse dotting the sky on their way to feast on the tasty delights of the city dump. They swooped in low over the housing project on Sampson Avenue splattering parked vehicles, buildings and residents with blotches of gull excrement. It was a truly unpleasant daily occurrence. The scavengers would light onto the plateau seeking some tasty morsel of rancid meat, even if it meant tearing into a plastic garbage bag to get at it.

Chapter Forty-Four:
"Hall of Fame"

As early as 1983, a group of music industry pundits set out to establish an organization to award the artists, media personalities and executives whose achievements and contributions to rock and roll music over the years warranted recognition. The group was led by Ahmet Ertegun, founder of Atlantic Records, Jan Wenner, publisher of *Rolling Stone* magazine, music attorneys Susan Evans and Allen Grubman along with noted music critic and manager Jon Landau and record executives Seymour Stein and Bob Krasnow. Together they created a non-profit organization that would become the Rock and Roll Hall of Fame Foundation.

By 1985, the Board of Directors was ready to implement their plans for an annual induction ceremony, as well as acquiring a permanent structure to serve as a museum, library and archive. Their original plan was to purchase a New York City brownstone for their purposes. Before they could do so however, a committee from the city of Cleveland, Ohio, approached the Foundation with an offer to build a major museum. The committee was headed by city officials and noted disk jockey Norm N. Nite. Armed with impressive plans and diagrams, the delegation presented a good argument as to why Cleveland should be selected. After all, wasn't it Alan Freed, a disc jockey on Cleveland radio, who first coined the term *rock and roll*?

Soon, other cities, New York, Philadelphia, New Orleans, San Francisco, along with Memphis and Chicago, all made offers to win the much coveted honor. A *USA Today* newspaper poll was conducted with Cleveland ranking first in the voting. In May of 1986 the Foundation announced Cleveland as the permanent home of the Rock and Roll Hall of Fame Museum.

A committee made up of rock historians selected a

group of nominees in a Performer's category. The criteria for this first crop of inductees was that they made their first recording prior to 1960, and that, in the eyes of the committee, they…"exhibited an influence and significance on the evolution of rock and roll music."

In addition to Performers, other categories included Nonperformers, Record Executives, Disc Jockeys, Songwriters and Producers whose contributions proved worthy of inclusion. Another category, Early Influences, included those whose music predated the rock era, but had an important impact on the genre. A special committee selected inductees in the Non-Performer and Early Influences categories. As for Performers, a list of over forty names were selected by the board and placed on a ballot sent to over two hundred members of a voting body of rock experts. Those receiving the highest number of votes were inducted.

And so, the inaugural Rock and Roll Hall of Fame class of 1986 included, a Lifetime Achievement Award to record producer and music critic John Hammond. For the Early Influences, R&B pioneers Jimmy Yancey, Jimmie Rogers and Robert Johnson, the man who legend said sold his soul to the devil for the ability to play R&B guitar, would be honored. In the Nonperformer category, awards went to Sam Phillips, owner of Sun Records in Memphis, and Cleveland disc jockey Alan Freed.

The Performers represented an elite group of men who forged the way in the early days; Ray Charles, Sam Cooke, Chuck Berry, James Brown, Fats Domino, Buddy Holly, the Everly Brothers, Jerry Lee Lewis, Little Richard, Elvis Presley and Teddy Boyette.

The Grand Ballroom of the Waldorf Astoria Hotel in New York City hosted the induction dinner and ceremony on the evening of October 23rd, 1986.

♫ ♫ ♫ ♫ ♫

Janet's prodding saw the Rabinowitz family arrive in plenty time for the sumptuous dinner. Joseph looked dashing in his custom-made tuxedo. His wife and daughter were elegantly decked out in stylish evening wear. The packed ballroom was electrified with excitement. Music stars and celebrities were everywhere. Many who knew one another by reputation only got the chance to shake the hands of their mentors and favorite artists, while others renewed past relationships.

There were impromptu moments. John Lennon's sons Julian and Sean posed for pictures with Billy Joel, Neil Young, Keith Richards and Don Everly. Paul Schaffer and the World's Most Dangerous Band, from the television talk show *Late Night with David Letterman*, provided music.

Though tuxedos and sequined gowns were in great abundance, the festivities had an air of irreverent and raucous behavior. This was further evidenced when Rolling Stones Guitarist Keith Richards came to the stage to induct Chuck Berry. He stripped off his tuxedo jacket to reveal a garish yellow leopard skin jacket underneath, to the sheer joy of the audience. Berry added to the fun by duck walking to the podium. This was, after all, rock and roll.

The night went on, emotionally charged by presenters and inductees alike. Radio greats Scott Muni and Norm N. Nite combined to pay homage to Alan Freed with Muni commenting, "Everyone in this room owes a lot to Alan Freed." The Disc Jockeys presented the award to Freed's son Lance.

A staff member came to the table and asked Joseph to follow him. It would soon be time for him to take the stage and induct Teddy Boyette.

"Do you have your notes?" Janet asked him as he stood to go. Joseph nodded.

"Good luck Daddy," Danielle told him.

Joseph smiled and was ushered off.

The two women in his life sat arm in arm in nervous

anticipation.

Ahmet Ertegun prepared the crowd for Joseph's appearance, speaking about his importance as the founder of Chanticleer Records. He remarked on how Joseph brought a totally unknown singer to New York and shaped him into one of rock and roll's most influential pioneers. "Now, to induct Teddy Boyette into the Rock and Roll Hall of Fame, please welcome, Joseph Rabinowitz."

Joseph was hardly aware of the applause that accompanied him to the podium. He reached into the inside pocket of his dinner jacket to produce his notes, written on several three-by-five index cards. He laid them out in front of him. During that time, Ertegun placed the statuette on the podium. Joseph picked it up and looked at it. It was made of a dark heavy metal. The base was a solid square block upon which stood a sleek slender human shape, its arms extended over the head to hold what appeared to be either a record or compact disc. It was beautiful in its simplicity.

"Thank you Ahmet. Thank you all," Joseph began. "To say that Teddy Boyette changed my life would be a gross oversimplification. He changed the lives of *everyone* he came in contact with because of his talent and his genius...his love of music and the love of the fans of his music. If I had anything to do with his success, it was merely as a catalyst to put him into the public eye. I didn't do it alone." His voice shook. "My music mentor Chanticleer Williams brought him to my attention. My business partner Leo Klein agreed to bring him in to record for our unknown, untried record label. My wife Janet helped write the songs that Teddy made his own and that his fans bought by the millions. My friend Jacob Miliewski helped get him on the air waves." Joseph paused to gather his emotions and get himself through the rest of his speech. He recalled Janet's words of long ago, "Teddy left us much too soon, like a comet burning out in the sky, leaving nothing but the bright trail of his path. He would have been proud, but humble, in receiving the honor you bestow on him tonight – just as I am proud to accept it on his behalf. I thank you all very much."

Joseph left the stage to a loud thunderous standing ovation. Many stopped him to shake his hand as he made his way back to his table. When he arrived, Janet and Danielle had tears in their eyes. Danielle jumped to embrace him. He handed her the statuette. "First chance we get you give that to TJ." Tears ran down her cheeks as Danielle sat in her chair admiring the award.

After kissing her husband hard, Janet whispered in his ear, "You were wonderful up there."

With the formalities of the awards presentation out of the way, it was time for music take over. An unrehearsed and totally impromptu jam session erupted. Inductees and presenters alike grabbed instruments and took to the stage in a superstar combination, the likes of which had never been seen before.

Chuck Berry started it all off with "Roll Over Beethoven," joined by Jerry Lee Lewis on boogie-woogie piano. Keith Richards and Neil Young took turns with Berry on guitar licks. "Johnny B. Goode" followed, this time Billy Joel helped on piano and Steve Winwood played the Hammond B-3 and provided backing vocals. Janet and Danielle joined scores of others kicking off their high heels and dancing up a storm. Jerry Lee belted out "Whole Lot of Shakin' Goin On." The star-studded ensemble showed the crowd why they were Hall of Fame caliber.

The grand finale proved truly special. John Fogarty, the former lead singer of Creedence Clearwater Revival, stepped up and led those on stage and nearly everyone else in the room in a rollicking rendition of his self-penned "Proud Mary."

Chapter Forty-Five:
"Aftermath"

"It's just not what I envisioned for your wedding," Janet told Danielle in one of those mother-daughter moments before a bride becomes a wife.

"I know," Danielle answered, "but...I mean West Point. It is kinda cool."

The US Attorney's office arranged for the use of the chapel at the West Point Military Academy for the nuptials of Danielle Rabinowitz and TJ Russell.

There were conditions. The event had to be kept secret and the guest list approved by the US Marshal's Service. A military chaplain performed the ceremony with a rabbi in attendance for a religious blessing. Shira Bar-On was maid of honor. Joseph did double duty by giving the bride away and acting as best man.

Weeks before the wedding, TJ testified at the trial that led to the conviction of five members of the Viola crime family. The trial lasted several months and was touch and go for a great while. A battery of defense attorneys attacked TJ's credibility as a witness. They argued he had no physical evidence of any such scheme to defraud the government. As one good mob lawyer objected, "In fact, Mr. Russell has in the past also made unsubstantiated claims that he is the son of a successful singer named Teddy Boyette."

But, the prosecutors had more. "Mr. Russell, did you on the evening of July eighth of last year perform a concert at Madison Square Garden?"

"Yes I did."

"And did anything unusual occur at the end of that concert?"

"Yes, as I came offstage, an older white haired gentleman approached me and handed me a large package."

"What was in the package?"

"File folders and ledger books."

The prosecutor picked up a ledger book from the stack of papers on the desk in front of him. "Is this one of the ledger books?"

"It appears to be, yes," TJ answered.

"Your honor, at this time the prosecution would like to enter into evidence..."

Another defense attorney stood, with his hand extended and pleaded with the judge. "Your honor, the defense reiterates its objection to place these items into evidence, we..."

"Objection overruled," the judge said loudly and firmly. "We've been over this counselor. The files stay."

The files contained damning information on the Viola family dating back over fifty years. There were records of bribes and payoffs to city, state and federal officials by name, date and amount. The connection between the mob and Alexis Records was clearly documented in the meticulous accounting methods of one, Max Seiderman. No one could say just how Max knew it was TJ who was going to testify against the record company and the mob. But, he proved to be an even *smarter Jew* than anyone ever gave him credit for.

The defense again objected, saying that since Max Seiderman had suddenly disappeared and could not be brought to testify, any evidence in reference to him also be excluded. Those objections were also overruled.

From then on, the outcome of the trial was never in doubt.

Though the wedding was a happy affair, it was also bittersweet. The extreme and stringent rules of the Federal Witness Protection Program dictated that TJ and Danielle be re-located to an undisclosed location. They were to be given new names and identities. Contact with anyone from their former lives, including parents, was strictly forbidden. This was to be the last night they would all be together.

As the hour grew late and Danielle changed her clothes, she spent some last moments with her mother. Joseph looked for TJ and found him in the quiet garden outside the chapel. Joseph had a guitar case in his hand as he approached.

"What's that?" TJ asked.

"Chanty's Senorita," Joseph answered offering him the case, "consider it a wedding present."

TJ shook his head. "Nah, Teddy woulda wanted you to have it." Joseph put the case on the ground and the two men sat on a wooden bench. "I'll make you a deal though. You keep the guitar and I'll hang on to that Hall of Fame *do-dad*. Only cause I figure before long you'll have one of those of your own."

"Not me, I don't deserve anything like that."

TJ shrugged. "I know an awful lot of people who would disagree with you on that score."

They saw Janet and Danielle approach arm in arm. Both of them were crying. The two men stood and shook hands.

"You take good care of my girl," Joseph said.

"I will," TJ replied.

Russell stepped aside to allow the family time to say goodbye. Danielle rushed into her father's arms. "I hate this." As they embraced, she spoke softly into his ear. "I spoke to Shira. She's gonna make sure we keep in touch no matter what the government says. You'll always know where I am." She let him go and stepped back. "I love you Daddy."

"I love you too baby. And don't worry...no matter where you are, every night we'll bounce you a kiss off the moon."

With that Danielle hugged and kissed her mother. They both wept uncontrollably. She and TJ walked away and Janet rushed to Joseph's side burying her face in his chest. He held her a long time until her shaking body stilled a bit. He glanced around taking in the beauty of the locale, the tree lined path to the rear of the chapel.

"You know," he said quietly, "I think we once wrote a song once about a place just like this."

Janet turned her head to the side. "I seem to remember that. Maybe we should write another one?"

"For our next comet?"

"It could happen, right?"

"A wise old man once said, *rock and roll will never die. It will always be.*"

The End